Basics
Of
Mid
Acts
Dispensationalism

By Terence D. McLean

Discerning the Times Publishing Co. Inc.

Scripture quotations in this book are from
the King James Bible,
God's perfectly preserved word.

Discerning The Times Publishing Co. Inc.
Post Office Box 87
Alpha OH 45301-0087

International Standard Book Number
0-9789863-1-8

Library of Congress Copyright
TX 6-486-899

Contents...

To The Reader...

John Nelson Darby was a dispensational pioneer who died in 1882, yet more than sixty of his books and booklets are still in print today.[1] You will never hear his voice and may not have known his name, but his books and his teachings endure.

This little book stands on Darby's shoulders and plainly declares Bible truths with which Darby struggled.

Dr. C. I. Scofield famously annotated his study Bible in 1917, and it is well said that no other study Bible has had the impact of the Scofield Study Bible.[2]

This little book benefits so very greatly from the scholarship of the Scofield board of editors that this book can correct their mistakes and misunderstandings.

More than a half century ago, Charles F. Baker assembled a six hundred eighty-eight page tome which still stands alone as a Dispensational Theology.[3]

This little book looks through the lens that Baker ground and sees with clarity a panorama of Bible doctrine that Baker perceived as shadows.

And so, many great dispensational teachers have contributed to this book and the level of dispensational understanding we all can now enjoy. Cornelius R. Stam, Ethelbert W. Bullinger, J. C. O'Hair, George Williams, and Robert Newell are most notable, but there are so many others.

It is not that "new" is necessarily better and it certainly is not that we are smarter or more spiritual: the reverse more likely is true. Perhaps it is that we can see more clearly because those who have gone before have shown us where to look.

This book is a simple primer in the dispensational school of thought that great men of days gone by diligently constructed. While you may not be familiar with the men who were the pioneers, we owe it to them and the message of grace to keep pressing on *"toward the mark for the prize of the high calling of God in Christ Jesus."* [4]

How wonderful it is that we now can see through the glass clearly. We are all members one of another in Jesus Christ according to the revelation of the mystery; and with the benefit of time and the hard work done in time past by great dispensational teachers, we now stand on solid ground with the Basics of Mid-Acts Dispensationalism.

---

1. Bible Truth Publishers, P.O. Box 649, Addison Illinois 60101
2. Oxford University Press, 2001 Evans Rd., Cary N.C. 27513
3. Grace Bible College Publications, 1011 Aldon Street S.W., Grand Rapids Michigan 49509
4. Philippians 3:14

Definitions . . .

Mid-Acts: Since the book of Acts has 28 chapters, the mid-point would be between chapters 14 and 15; so the term Mid-Acts is not arithmetically correct. Mid-Acts, in the dispensational context, refers to the 9th chapter because that is when Jesus Christ began His dealings with the Apostle Paul. Some might also point to the 13th chapter because it is there that Paul first makes a statement that some in Israel considered worthy of death:

> *Acts 13:38-39: Be it known unto you therefore, men and brethren, that through this man is preached unto you the forgiveness of sins: And by him all that believe are justified from all things, from which ye could not be justified by the law of Moses.*

Forgiveness through Christ, rather than by performance of Moses' law, was the message the Lord entrusted to Paul, hence the doctrine which would follow from that would properly be called **Pauline**.

Dispensationalism has been defined by many authors but seldom will you ever read an objective definition, since the topic is not without controversy. Those who oppose the concept reveal their predilection in their definition, as does Dr. Charles Caudill Ryrie.[1] Those who favor the concept are no more objective, with a notable example being Charles F. Baker.[2]

If we allow the Bible to be our authority, it is readily apparant that God has not always dispensed the same information to the
same people at all times.[3]

Significantly, the Bible contains information which everyone could know since
the world began; and the Bible also contains
information which no one could know until
Christ imparted it to Paul:

> Acts 3:21: Whom the heaven must re-
> ceive until the times of restitution of all
> things, which God hath **spoken** by the
> mouth of all his holy prophets **since the**
> **world began.**

> Romans 16:25: Now to him that is of
> power to stablish you according to my
> gospel, and the preaching of Jesus
> Christ, according to the revelation of
> the mystery, which was kept **secret**
> **since the world began,**

The importance of Mid-Acts Pauline
dispensationism lies in the differentiation between that which had been prophesied and
that which was a mystery until Christ revealed it to the apostle Paul. Some of the
differences are minor, and this book will not
major on the minors. Rather, presented here
are the basics of Mid-Acts Dispensationalism.

---

1. Dispensationalism, Charles C. Ryrie, Moody Press, Chapter eleven

2. Dispensational Theology, Charles F. Baker, Grace Bible
Press, pages 1-3

3. *Hebrews 1:1 God, who at sundry times and in divers
manners spake in time past unto the fathers by the prophets*

Rightly Dividing

is not optional...

II Timothy 2:15 is not a suggestion:
Study to shew thyself approved unto God, a workman that needeth not to be ashamed, rightly dividing the word of truth.

That the Bible has divisions in it cannot be argued: there is the Old Testament and the New Testament; and everyone would agree to those divisions.

Amazingly, most everyone would say that the Old Testament begins with Genesis chapter one and that the New Testament begins with the first chapter of Matthew; and that means most everyone would be wrong.

Since the Old Testament is the giving of the law, that could not begin until the covenant of the law actually is delivered in Exodus 19.[1] Since the New Testament could not take effect without the death of the testator, that could not be before Christ dies on the cross.[2]

From this we see that our ideas as to where the Old and New Testaments start were not a function of Bible study, and so we must allow the Bible to correct our wrong thinking. Those title pages in our Bibles announcing "Old Testament" and "New Testament" were placed in a convenient location by the Bible publishers, but the placement of those pages taught us wrong things about Bible doctrine.

Additionally, we will see that Christ gave instructions to the apostle Paul which are neither New nor Old Testament doctrine, but rather according to a mystery which had been hidden since before the world began.

Recognizing this mystery and respecting the importance of this mystery to God's wise plan to glorify Christ both in heaven and on the Earth is the key to understanding the Bible and is the focus of this book. ·

None of us would want to be guilty of *"wrongly dividing the word of truth"* or of rejecting *"all the counsel of God."* [3] We are guilty of both of those indiscretions if we fail to recognize and respect the revelation of the mystery which the Lord Jesus Christ delivered to the apostle Paul beginning in the ninth chapter of the book of the Acts of the apostles.

---

1. *Exodus 19:5 Now therefore, if ye will obey my voice indeed, and keep my covenant, then ye shall be a peculiar treasure unto me above all people: for all the earth is mine:*

2. *Matthew 26:28 For this is my blood of the new testament, which is shed for many for the remission of sins.*

3. *Timothy 2:15 Study to shew thyself approved unto God, a workman that needeth not to be ashamed, rightly dividing the word of truth.*

Acts 20:27 For I have not shunned to declare unto you all the counsel of God.

We must Recognize and Respect the Revelation of the Mystery...

The Bible declares that Jesus Christ revealed the mystery to the Apostle Paul:

In Ephesians 3:3, Paul writes *"that by revelation he made known unto me the mystery; (as I wrote afore in few words,"*

We read about the mystery in Paul's writings, but for more than four thousand years it *"hath been hid from ages and from generations, but now is made manifest to his saints,"* according to Colossians 1:26.

None of the twelve apostles was privy to this mystery as Paul declares *"I neither received it of man, neither was I taught it, but by the revelation of Jesus Christ,"* according to Galatians 1:12.

Before the creation, before Adam and Eve, the Godhead of Father, Son and Spirit had planned this mystery and ordained when Jesus Christ, God manifest in the flesh, would *"speak the wisdom of God in a mystery, even the hidden wisdom, which God ordained before the world unto our glory:"* (I Corinthians 2:7).

We are to engage in the *"preaching of Jesus Christ, according to the revelation of the mystery, which was kept secret since the world began,"* (Romans 16:25), which clearly differs from Peter's message which was *"spoken by the mouth of all his holy prophets since the world began,"* according to Acts 3:21.

Although most Christians think of "stewardship" in terms of money and other resources, we are to be *"stewards of the mysteries of God"* and faithful stewards at that. (I Corinthians 4:1-2)

"I would not, brethren, that ye should be ignorant of this mystery, lest ye should be wise in your own conceits," (Romans 11:25) and so we cannot be pleasing to God by choosing to be ignorant of mystery truth. The Lord stopped winking at ignorance back in Acts 17:30[1]; and so we must get back to the basics, the three r's: Recognize and Respect the Revelation of the mystery.

Now that we have recognized the existence of this mystery and that it was given by Christ to Paul, we next must learn the content of this revelation. With that knowledge, we will come to respect the importance and impact of the mystery on our biblical understanding.

The "Revelation of the Mystery" is a term which describes the body of new information which Christ imparted to Paul; and there are six most important aspects to this mystery truth.

1. Israel is blind and fallen, and as a result, a new salvation program comes to Gentiles:
Romans 11:11:...through their fall

salvation is come unto the Gentiles...

Romans 11:25: For I would not, brethren, that ye should be ignorant of this mystery, lest ye should be wise in your own conceits; that blindness in part is happened to Israel, until the fulness of the Gentiles be come in.

2. God's dealings with humanity changes to... "the dispensation of the grace of God which is given me [Paul] to youward" (Ephesians 3:2) ... "Which in other ages was not made known unto the sons of men, as it is now revealed unto his holy apostles" (Ephesians 3:5) apart from the law "for ye are not under the law, but under grace." (Romans 6:14) and without Israel "for I perceive that God is no respecter of persons:" (Acts 10:34).

3. Humanity's dealings with God change because of "the mystery which hath been hid from ages and from generations, but now is made manifest to his saints:" (Colossians 1:26) which entails a new relationship with Christ because God now has made "known what is the riches of the glory of this mystery among the Gentiles; which is Christ in you, the hope of glory:" (Colossians 1:27)

4. The focus becomes a new creature (the body of Christ) with Christ as the head, rather than Israel's kingdom over which Christ will be king:

   II Corinthians 5:17: Therefore if any man be in Christ, he is a new creature: old things are passed away; behold, all things are become new.

   Colossians 1:18: And he is the head of the body, the church: who is the beginning, the firstborn from the dead; that in all things he might have the preeminence.

5. The Lord has us here on Earth as His ambassadors:

   II Corinthians 5:20: Now then we are ambassadors for Christ, as though God did beseech you by us:

   And the Lord would have us to see souls saved and saints edified: I Timothy 2:4.

6. Rather than ruling on the Earth with the tribes of Israel, we will meet Jesus Christ in heavenly places:

   I Corinthians 15:51: Behold, I shew you a mystery; We shall not all sleep, but we shall all be changed,

   I Thessalonians 4:13: But I would not have you to be ignorant, brethren, concerning them which

are asleep, that ye sorrow not, even as others which have no hope.
I Thessalonians 4:16-17: For the Lord himself shall descend from heaven with a shout, with the voice of the archangel, and with the trump of God: and the dead in Christ shall rise first: Then we which are alive and remain shall be caught up together with them in the clouds, to meet the Lord in the air: and so shall we ever be with the Lord.

Now that we have recognized the existence of the mystery and that it was given by Christ to Paul, and now that we have briefly identified the six points of doctrinal content, we are prepared to learn to respect the importance and impact of the mystery on our biblical understanding. That will entail a study of the Basics of Mid-Acts Dispensationalism.

---

1. *Acts 17:30 And the times of this ignorance God winked at; but now commandeth all men every where to repent:*

Israel and the Body of Christ are different...

Rather than Christ's twelve apostles sent to Israel, Paul says *"I am the apostle of the Gentiles, I magnify mine office:"* (Romans 11:13), *"the minister of Jesus Christ to the Gentiles"* (Romans 15:16), *"the prisoner of Jesus Christ for you Gentiles"* (Ephesians 3:1);* and Paul alone refers to this present time period in which we live as the *"dispensation of the grace of God"* (Ephesians 3:2)

Instead of Israel's being *"...for a light of the Gentiles"* (Isaiah 42:6) Paul alone states the fact that *"a dispensation of the gospel is committed unto me."* (I Corinthians 9:17), and rather than following in the footsteps of Christ, Paul calls himself the *"pattern to them which should hereafter believe on him to life everlasting."* (I Timothy 1:16).

God sent His Son: subsequently, His Son sent Paul, signaling a change in God's administration (no doubt much better said, "dispensation"). In this present dispensation of grace, salvation now is being dispensed (or administered) to uncircumcised Gentiles by grace through faith alone without the works of the law:

Ephesians 2:8-9: For by grace are ye

saved through faith; and that not of yourselves: it is the gift of God: Not of works, lest any man should boast.

Titus 3:5: Not by works of righteousness which we have done, but according to his mercy he saved us,

Israel found righteous standing by performing in accordance with the law:

Deuteronomy 6:25: And it shall be our righteousness, if we observe to do all these commandments before the LORD our God, as he hath commanded us.

The Lord Jesus Christ Himself affirmed the need for performance when He talked about: *"they that have done good, unto the resurrection of life; and they that have done evil, unto the resurrection of damnation." (John 5:29).*

Clearly there has been a dispensational change of administration in that salvation now is *"...to him that worketh not, but believeth on him that justifieth the ungodly, his faith is counted for righteouness." (Romans 4:5)*

Grace and works cannot be combined or accumulated because they are mutually exclusive according to *Romans 11:6: "...if by grace, then is it no more of works: otherwise grace is no more grace. But if it be of works, then it is no more grace: otherwise work is no more work."*

Clearly, there has been a dispensational change of administration which no one saw coming at the time and many have yet to see even today.

However, until God revealed this mystery to Paul, this dispensation of grace in which we live, and its doctrinal content had never been revealed. Paul clearly states that this present dispensation was not previously *"made known"* (revealed) unto the sons of men:

> *Ephesians 3:1-6: For this cause I Paul, the prisoner of Jesus Christ for you Gentiles, If ye have heard of the dispensation of the grace of God which is given me to you-ward: How that by revelation he made known unto me the mystery; (as I wrote afore in few words, Whereby, when ye read, ye may understand my knowledge in the mystery of Christ) Which in other ages was not made known unto the sons of men, as it is now revealed unto his holy apostles and prophets by the Spirit; That the Gentiles should be fellowheirs, and of the same body, and partakers of his promise in Christ by the gospel:*

The revelation of the mystery in this dispensation is as important to see and understand as seeing and understanding the iceberg would have been for the captain of the Titanic; and the consequences of not knowing are even more dire, for God's eternal truth requires right division.

The Bible often refers to Israel as the "circumcision" because of the covenant of circumcision which God instituted. Gentiles often are referred to as the "uncircumcision" and strangers because Gentiles had no such covenant and were strangers to it.

> *Ephesians 2:12: That at that time ye*

were without Christ, being aliens from the commonwealth of Israel, and strangers from the covenants of promise, having no hope, and without God in the world:

The simple difference between the "circumcision" and the "uncircumcision" stands as proof that this dispensation of the mystery could not have been a subject during the times targeting the "circumcision" because during those times the "uncircumcision" had no hope.

Genesis 17:14: And the uncircumcised man child whose flesh of his foreskin is not circumcised, that soul shall be cut off from his people; he hath broken my covenant.

Exodus 12:48: And when a stranger shall sojourn with thee, and will keep the passover to the Lord, let all his males be circumcised, and then let him come near and keep it; and he shall be as one that is born in the land: for no uncircumcised person shall eat thereof.

Ezekiel 44:7-9: In that ye have brought into my sanctuary strangers, uncircumcised in heart, and uncircumcised in flesh, to be in my sanctuary, to pollute it, even my house, when ye offer my bread, the fat and the blood, and they have broken my covenant because of all your abominations. And ye have not kept the charge of mine holy things: but ye have set keepers of my charge in my sanctuary for yourselves. Thus saith the Lord God; No stranger, uncir-

cumcised in heart, nor uncircumcised in flesh, shall enter into my sanctuary, of any stranger that is among the children of Israel.

The body of prophetic information in the Bible constitutes that which was well known: *"As he spake by the mouth of his holy prophets, which have been <u>since the world began:"</u> (Luke 1:70)* and nothing had changed well into Peter's ministry: *"Whom the heaven must receive until the times of restitution of all things, which God hath spoken by the mouth of all his holy prophets <u>since the world began."</u> (Acts 3:21).*

Christ revealed new information to Paul and so Paul has some things very different to say:

> *Colossians 1:25-27: Whereof I am made a minister, according to the dispensation of God which is given to me for you, to fulfil the word of God; Even the mystery which hath been hid from ages and from generations, but now is made manifest to his saints: To whom God would make known what is the riches of the glory of this mystery among the Gentiles; which is Christ in you, the hope of glory:*

These verses and those in Ephesians chapter three prove that this present dispensation was made known to Paul after having been hidden and never foretold in prophecy. To miss this as one navigates through God's word inevitably leads to shipwreck. Paul's writings alone contain God's dispensational information for the Body of Christ, information which had been hidden from God's prophetic administration involving Israel.

When the Titanic hit the iceberg and sank, it was said that 1523 souls were lost: that would be doctrinally true only for the unsaved victims of that disaster. Meanwhile, every soul that fails to trust the gospel of the grace of God preached according to the revelation of the mystery is eternally shipwrecked and lost in hell. Rightly dividing is not optional.

The Lord Jesus Christ and His twelve apostles preached to Israel, and the content of the message was identified as "the gospel of the kingdom."

> *Matthew 4:23: And Jesus went about all Galilee, teaching in their synagogues, and preaching the gospel of the kingdom, and healing all manner of sickness and all manner of disease among the people.*
>
> *Matthew 9:35: And Jesus went about all the cities and villages, teaching in their synagogues, and preaching the gospel of the kingdom, and healing every sickness and every disease among the people.*
>
> *Matthew 24:14: And this gospel of the kingdom shall be preached in all the world for a witness unto all nations; and then shall the end come.*

It is very important to note that the gospel of the kingdom did not include the cross, Christ's death, burial and resurrection, as that information was still hidden from understanding.

Mark 9:31-32: For he taught his disciples, and said unto them, The Son of man is delivered into the hands of men, and they shall kill him; and after that he is killed, he shall rise the third day. But they understood not that saying, and were afraid to ask him.

Luke 9:44-45: Let these sayings sink down into your ears: for the Son of man shall be delivered into the hands of men. But they understood not this saying, and it was hid from them, that they perceived it not: and they feared to ask him of that saying.

John 20:9: For as yet they knew not the scripture, that he must rise again from the dead.

The apostle Peter had been given the keys to the prophetic program; and yet when the prince of the apostles was told about the cross, Peter tried to prevent the crucifixion from taking place. Since Peter, the Lord and the rest of the apostles had been preaching the gospel of the kingdom for some time, it is obvious that the gospel of the kingdom could not have included the cross, the death, burial and resurrection of Christ.

Matthew 16:21-22: From that time forth began Jesus to shew unto his disciples, how that he must go unto Jerusalem, and suffer many things of the elders and chief priests and scribes, and be killed, and be raised again the third day. Then Peter took him, and began to rebuke him, saying, Be it far from thee, Lord: this shall not be unto thee.

Unlike the gospel of the kingdom, Paul declares that his gospel, the gospel of the grace of God, the preaching of Jesus Christ according to the revelation of the mystery, is all about Calvary's cross.

I Corinthians 15:1-4: Moreover, brethren, I declare unto you the gospel which I preached unto you, which also ye have received, and wherein ye stand; By which also ye are saved, if ye keep in memory what I preached unto you, unless ye have believed in vain. For I delivered unto you first of all that which I also received, how that Christ died for our sins according to the scriptures; And that he was buried, and that he rose again the third day according to the scriptures:

Since the focus of the gospel of the kingdom is the kingdom of that gospel, there can be no mistaking that it belonged to Israel and had been prophesied.

Luke 1:68-70:   Blessed be the Lord God of Israel; for he hath visited and redeemed his people, And hath raised up an horn of salvation for us in the house of his servant David; As he spake by the mouth of his holy prophets, which have been since the world began:

In contrast to this present dispensation of grace, the gospel of the kingdom was not a mystery at all, because prophecy clearly stated that God's kingdom was to be established literally at some future point, with Jerusalem at its center.

The focus of God's prophetic program for Israel, the focus of the gospel of the kingdom, was and will again be Christ ruling on this Earth:

> *Daniel 7:14: And there was given him dominion, and glory, and a kingdom, that all people, nations, and languages, should serve him: his dominion is an everlasting dominion, which shall not pass away, and his kingdom that which shall not be destroyed.*
>
> *Revelation 11:15: And the seventh angel sounded; and there were great voices in heaven, saying, The kingdoms of this world are become the kingdoms of our Lord, and of his Christ; and he shall reign for ever and ever.*

The focus of the gospel of the grace of God preached according to the revelation of the mystery is not about a physical kingdom on Earth, but spiritual blessings in heavenly places:

> *Ephesians 1:3: Blessed be the God and Father of our Lord Jesus Christ, who hath blessed us with all spiritual blessings in heavenly places in Christ:*
>
> *I Corinthians 15:40: There are also celestial bodies, and bodies terrestrial: but the glory of the celestial is one, and the glory of the terrestrial is another.*
>
> *I Corinthians 15:47: The first man is of the earth, earthy; the second man is the Lord from heaven.*

Because Israel rejected Christ and His prophetic message of the kingdom, Israel fell and the kingdom ceased to be *"at hand."*

Because Israel has fallen, salvation is come to the Gentiles, not with the gospel of the rejected kingdom, but with the gospel of the grace of God.

Because prophecies concerning Gentile salvation through the glorification of Israel would be through the kingdom gospel, they could not be the same as Gentile salvation which comes through the fall of Israel. That means there are prophecies for Israel that have yet to be fulfilled; and just as the mystery program was not operating during Israel's time, Israel's program is not operating now. When the part of the mystery program involving the removal of the Body of Christ into heavenly places occurs, God then will complete Israel's prophetic program.

Because salvation of uncircumcised Gentiles never was foretold or accommodated during the law program or during the earthly ministry of Christ, this present dispensation involves an administration of God that was unprophesied.

Dispensationalism simply recognizes the differences between Israel and the Body of Christ.

Dispensationalism respects the doctrinal impact of the differences between Israel and the Body of Christ and responds accordingly.

Dispensationalism accepts what the Bible says but also respects to whom it says it.

Dispensationalists realize that God has different things to say to the Body of Christ than He had said to Israel, just as certainly as Israel's gospel of the kingdom did not include the preaching of the cross.

Dispensationalists recognize that while all God's Bible is for our learning, not all of God's word is written to us for our doctrinal application.

More specifically, Mid-Acts Dispensationalism is based upon the fact that the present body of Christ began with the apostle Paul, when he was saved in Acts chapter nine and as the Lord gave to Paul the revelation of the mystery which had been so long hidden.

Before he met the Lord Jesus Christ, Paul had been named Saul, and Saul was a Gentile (Roman) following the Jewish religion (Sanhedrin).

> *Acts 21:39 But Paul said, I am a man which am a Jew of Tarsus...*
>
> *Acts 22:25 ...Is it lawful for you to scourge a man that is a Roman, and uncondemned?*
>
> *Philippians 3:5 Circumcised the eighth day, of the stock of Israel, of the tribe of Benjamin, an Hebrew of the Hebrews; as touching the law, a Pharisee;*

When Christ saved Saul and gave him the revelation of the mystery, Saul became Paul, a new creature, Jew and Gentile in one body, the body of Christ, in which there is neither Jew nor Greek.

Israel and the body of Christ are different.

"Gospel of the Kingdom"
"Gospel of God's Grace"
...are different

While sincere people will tell you that everyone in the Bible gets saved the same way, such is not the testimony of scripture.

While popular preachers proclaim that "everyone in the Old Testament was saved by looking forward to the cross just as everyone in the New Testament is saved by looking backward to the cross," such is not the testimony of scripture.

While there may be a visceral response to first hearing that there is more than one plan of salvation in the Bible, it should not be our "gut" but our careful study of God's words that we trust.

While this chapter may elicit a "knee jerk reaction," come let us reason together and see what the Bible has to say, remembering that even Paul kicked against the truth until the Lord showed Paul a more excellent way.

The books of Matthew, Mark, Luke and John are referred to as the "four gospels," but that is not what we are talking about here. The word "gospel" means "good news" and our interest is in noticing that there are several messages of "good news" in the Bible, and the good news message in the four gospels is that of the kingdom.

Our "good news" gospel message is that Christ died for our sins.

> *Moreover, brethren, I declare unto you the gospel...*
>
> *By which also ye are saved...*
>
> *...how that Christ died for our sins according to the scriptures;*
>
> *And that he was buried, and that he rose again the third day according to the scriptures. (I Corinthians 15:1-4)*

Righteous standing for Adam and Eve involved avoiding a particular tree: *"But of the tree of the knowledge of good and evil, thou shalt not eat of it: for in the day that thou eatest thereof thou shalt surely die." (Genesis 2:17)*

Righteous standing was accorded Noah because he built the ark: *"But Noah found grace in the eyes of the LORD." (Genesis 6:8)*

Note the combination of Noah's faith with the required performance required of him:

> *Genesis 7:5 And Noah did according unto all that the LORD commanded him.*
>
> *Hebrews 11:7 By faith Noah, being warned of God of things not seen as yet, moved with fear, prepared an ark to the saving of his house; by the which he condemned the world, and became heir of the righteousness which is by faith.*

Righteous standing was imputed to Abraham because by faith Abraham believed the covenant promises which Jehovah God had given: *"For what saith the scripture? Abraham believed God, and it was counted unto him for righteousness." (Romans 4:3)*

Righteousness was available to Moses and the children of Israel contingent upon performance of the commandments of God: *"And the LORD commanded us to do all these statutes, to fear the LORD our God, for our good always, that he might preserve us alive, as it is at this day. And it shall be our righteousness, if we observe to do all these commandments before the LORD our God, as he hath commanded us." (Deuteronomy 6:24-25).*

Paul reaffirms that under the law righteous standing was the product of prescribed performance: *"For Moses describeth the righteousness which is of the law, That the man which doeth those things shall live by them,"* yet according to the revelation of the mystery Christ gave to Paul *"...Christ is the end of the law for righteousness to every one that believeth." (Romans 10:5, 10:4)*

Significantly, *"The law and the prophets were until John: since that time the kingdom of God is preached, and every man presseth into it." (Luke 16:16);* and so while the kingdom being at hand is added, there is nothing in the verse to indicate that either the law or the prophetic doctrines had ceased. Rather, *"Think not that I am come to destroy the law, or the prophets: I am not come to destroy, but to fulfil." (Matthew 5:17)* for *"...God sent forth his Son, made of a woman, made under the law,"* (Galatians

4:4)

Eternal life was the subject of a question asked of the Lord Jesus Christ in *Matthew 19:16: "And, behold, one came and said unto him, Good Master, what good thing shall I do, that I may have eternal life?"*

It is important to notice what the Lord did not say: He did not say, "Believe on the Lord Jesus Christ and thou shalt be saved." He did not say, "By grace are ye saved through faith." He did not say, "Salvation is a gift of God, not of works lest any man should boast."

What Jesus Christ in fact did say was perfectly consistent with the required performance under the law program: *"...but if thou wilt enter into life, keep the commandments." (Matthew 19:17)*

Prior to the Lord's crucifixion, the apostles never understood that Jesus had to die, much less that He would die for the sins of uncircumcised Gentiles. What the apostles did not know, however, did not preclude their preaching the "gospel of the kingdom" because the gospel of the kingdom does not include Christ's death on Calvary's cruel cross.

Matthew 4:23: And Jesus went about all Galilee, teaching in their synagogues, and preaching the gospel of the kingdom, and healing all manner of sickness and all manner of disease among the people.
Matthew 9:35: And Jesus went about all the cities and villages, teaching in

their synagogues, and preaching the gospel of the kingdom, and healing every sickness and every disease among the people.

Jesus and His apostles meant what they were saying: the kingdom was literally at hand, and the culmination of the prophetic program was soon to be. This explains why physical healing is always associated with the gospel of the kingdom, as Israel would soon be the *"chosen generation, a royal priesthood, an holy nation, a peculiar people;"* (I Peter 2:9) To be a priest in the holy nation Israel requires that a person be physically whole *(Leviticus 21:17-23),* and that is why physical healing is always associated with Israel's gospel of the kingdom.

John the Baptist first began preaching that the kingdom of heaven was "at hand" in *Matthew 3:1-2: "In those days came John the Baptist, preaching in the wilderness of Judaea, And saying, Repent ye: for the kingdom of heaven is at hand."*

Jesus Himself also preached, *"Repent: for the kingdom of heaven is at hand",* (Matthew 4:17); and just six verses later, this message that Jesus preached is properly referred to as "the gospel of the kingdom", *"And Jesus went about all Galilee, teaching in their synagogues, and preaching the gospel of the kingdom, and healing all manner of sickness and all manner of disease among the people."* (Matthew 4:23) Preaching that the kingdom was at hand and granting physical healing in preparation for that kingdom, then, is what constitutes preaching the gospel of the kingdom.

While it is true that Jesus spoke of His death, burial and resurrection several times in the four gospels, the apostles never understood, and it was hidden from them. It would be gross error to read into the gospels that which was not understood:

> *Luke 9:44-45: Let these sayings sink down into your ears: for the Son of man shall be delivered into the hands of men. But they understood not this saying, and it was hid from them, that they perceived it not: and they feared to ask him of that saying.*

Mark also demonstrates that while he and the rest of the disciples were preaching the gospel of the kingdom they did not understand what would become the elements of the gospel of the grace of God: Christ's death, burial and resurrection:

> *Mark 9:30-32: And they departed thence, and passed through Galilee; and he would not that any man should know it. For he taught his disciples, and said unto them, The Son of man is delivered into the hands of men, and they shall kill him; and after that he is killed, he shall rise the third day. But they understood not that saying, and were afraid to ask him.*

There are many other passages documenting the fact that the twelve apostles never realized Jesus would die on the cross only to resurrect from the dead, as they went forth preaching the gospel of the kingdom. One of the most illuminating involves

Peter: already preaching the gospel of the kingdom, already in possession of the keys to the kingdom as well as binding and losing power, Peter attempted to prevent the crucifixion:

Matthew 16:21-23: From that time forth began Jesus to shew unto his disciples, how that he must go unto Jerusalem, and suffer many things of the elders and chief priests and scribes, and be killed, and be raised again the third day. Then Peter took him, and began to rebuke him, saying, Be it far from thee, Lord: this shall not be unto thee.

Just prior to the actual event's taking place, the apostles still lacked understanding:

Luke 18:31-34: Then he took unto him the twelve, and said unto them, Behold, we go up to Jerusalem, and all things that are written by the prophets concerning the Son of man shall be accomplished. For he shall be delivered unto the Gentiles, and shall be mocked, and spitefully entreated, and spitted on: And they shall scourge him, and put him to death: and the third day he shall rise again. And they understood none of these things: and this saying was hid from them, neither knew they the things which were spoken.

Even when the Lord was taken to be crucified, Peter still did not realize that Christ would die and be resurrected. Otherwise, he would not have cut off the ear of the high priest's servant in a failed attempt to prevent the crucifixion:

> *John 18:10-11: Then Simon Peter having a sword drew it, and smote the high priest's servant, and cut off his right ear. The servant's name was Malchus. Then said Jesus unto Peter, Put up thy sword into the sheath: the cup which my Father hath given me, shall I not drink it?*

Even immediately after the resurrection had taken place, there was neither understanding nor rejoicing.

> *John 20:9: For as yet they knew not the scripture, that he must rise again from the dead.*

Paul reveals that the mystery was hidden from the princes of this world so that the Lord could confound His enemies:

> *I Corinthians 2:7-8: But we speak the wisdom of God in a mystery, even the hidden wisdom, which God ordained before the world unto our glory: Which none of the princes of this world knew: for had they known it, they would not have crucified the Lord of glory.*

This makes it very clear as we read through the four gospels that neither Christ nor His apostles could have been preaching the gospel by which we are saved because the gospel of the kingdom they preached does not include the doctrinal information by which we are saved, namely, faith in Christ's death, burial and resurrection on our behalf.

> *Moreover, brethren, I declare unto you the gospel...*

By which also ye are saved...
For I delivered unto you first of all that which I also received, how that Christ died for our sins according to the scriptures; that he was buried, and that he rose again the third day according to the scriptures: (I Corinthians 15:1-4)

After preaching the gospel of the kingdom for more than three years it remained true that the people of the four gospels did not know what Paul would learn from the resurrected Christ:

The fact that Christ *"...was delivered for our offences, and was raised again for our justification."* (Romans 4:25) was mystery information delivered to Paul, information the apostles never comprehended.

When this dispensation and its doctrines operating according to the revelation of the mystery concludes, God will be at liberty to complete Israel's kingdom program, as prophesied:

Micah 4:1-3:   But in the last days it shall come to pass, that the mountain of the house of the LORD shall be established in the top of the mountains, and it shall be exalted above the hills; and people shall flow unto it. And many nations shall come, and say, Come, and let us go up to the mountain of the LORD, and to the house of the God of Jacob; and he will teach us of his ways, and we will walk in his paths: for the law shall go forth of Zion, and the word of the LORD from Jerusalem. And he shall judge among many people, and rebuke strong nations afar off; and they shall beat their swords into plowshares, and their spears into pruninghooks: nation shall not lift up a sword against nation, neither shall they learn war any more.

Jesus said *"And this gospel of the kingdom shall be preached in all the world for a witness unto all nations; and then shall the end come." (Matthew 24:14)* And, the end has not yet come.

Paul said *"...the hope of the gospel, which ye have heard, and which was preached to every creature which is under heaven; whereof I Paul am made a minister;" (Colossians 1:23).* And since the end did not come when every creature had heard, clearly the gospel Paul preached was not the gospel of the kingdom but rather *"the gospel of the grace of God." (Acts 20:24)*

Today, in this present dispensation of grace, the kingdom is no longer being offered to Israel, as they rejected their kingdom and crucified their King. God's prophesied kingdom temporarily has been set aside, and it is no longer at hand. The gospel of the kingdom that the apostles were preaching does not apply to this present dispensation, because there is no salvation today apart from the gospel of the grace of God.

The gospel of the kingdom and the gospel of the grace of God are different.

We cannot read back into scripture that which is revealed later.

The reader of the Bible often approaches the word of God as if it were, as so many have said, "God's love letter from heaven," the idea being that every word is expressly ours to believe and cherish. We are right to believe and cherish every word of God, but we would be terribly wrong to think that all of the doctrines contained in the Bible were for us to perform: trying to *"drink any deadly thing" (Mark 16:17)* or stoning the people who don't observe the Sabbath (Numbers 15:32-36) for example.

> *God, who at sundry times and in divers manners spake in time past unto the fathers by the prophets, (Hebrews 1:1)*

From this one verse we see God speaking to the fathers and to no one else. We see God speaking at sundry (various) times in divers (different) manners, and we must learn to respect those variations.

The reader of the Bible often starts at Genesis and reads through to the end of the Revelation, accumulating everything read into one belief system. Actually, few things could be more wrong, as the Bible contains progressive revelation, with newer information often supplanting the old.

While in the garden of Eden, God required that Adam and Eve be vegetarians:

Genesis 1:29: And God said, Behold, I have given you every herb bearing seed, which is upon the face of all the earth, and every tree, in the which is the fruit of a tree yielding seed; to you it shall be for meat.

As yet, sin had not entered, there was no curse upon the Earth, and so God had Adam caring for the animals, not eating them.

Romans 5:12: Wherefore, as by one man sin entered into the world, and death by sin; and so death passed upon all men, for that all have sinned:

With the advent of sin and humanity's expulsion from the garden, the earth was cursed and God killed an animal to clothe Adam and Eve. Things had changed.

Subsequently:

Genesis 9:3: Every moving thing that liveth shall be meat for you; even as the green herb have I given you all things.

God's purpose in changing the dietary program was to illustrate that the wages of sin is death, to demonstrate that what went on in the garden had been supplanted with a new program. Practically speaking, chasing down animals for food would encourage people to spread out around the globe, since the garden was now off limits.

Most everyone knows that Jehovah God gave Israel a dietary program in which were acceptable clean animals and forbidden unclean animals. This would be a third set of dietary instructions, and clearly they cannot be accumulated or combined; they must be rightly divided.

Even though Moses wrote the first five books of the Bible, which means that Moses wrote all three of the dietary programs contained in those books, Moses was required to obey what was written in Leviticus, not what was written in Genesis. Moses could not pick his favorite and disregard the others. Moses could not accumulate and combine the programs, as they were mutually exclusive. Moses had to respect progressive revelation, for even though God had inspired the one man, Moses, and Moses had written the first five books of the Bible, clearly *"God.. at sundry times and in divers manners spake..." (Hebrews 1:1)* New information had supplanted that which had been in place previously; and it would have been wrong to read Genesis as if it said the same thing as Leviticus and vice versa.

Our dietary instructions are different still, and we have no more authority to pick a favorite or accumulate doctrines than did Moses. Paul tells us that *"...the Spirit speaketh expressly, that in the latter times some shall depart from the faith, giving heed to seducing spirits, and doctrines of devils; ...commanding to abstain from meats, which God hath created to be received with thanksgiving of them which believe and know the truth. For every creature of God is good, and nothing to be refused, if it be received with thanksgiving:" (I Timothy 4:1-4)* Amazing and illuminating: Adam and

Eve were told by God to be vegetarians, and that same instruction is a *"doctrine of devils"* in Paul's letter to Timothy. Even under the law in Leviticus, certain meats were forbidden and so *"every creature of God"* was not good back then, as they are said to be in First Timothy.

Understanding this concept of progressive revelation, whereby doctrines do not accumulate and combining doctrines is wrong, prepares our minds to consider again just how wrong it is to read back into a text those doctrines that are not actually revealed until later.

The content of a well-known Messianic prophecy provides an excellent example, illustrating this truth:

Although Isaiah chapter fifty-three is a prophecy that Christ was to be "wounded" for someone's transgressions, and that He would be "bruised" for someone's iniquities, our present understanding of this prophecy is based upon subsequent explanations revealed in the scriptures, because the passage in Isaiah is not very specific. While the apostles undoubtedly were familiar with this Old Testament passage, its application was hidden from them as they went forth preaching the gospel of the kingdom. Even though we now know that Isaiah chapter fifty-three is a prophecy about the crucifixion of Jesus (which Philip explained to the Ethiopian Eunuch in Acts chapter eight), we have the advantage of both New Testament and Pauline scriptures to explain this. The apostles, though, did not yet possess this understanding prior to the Lord's resurrection. It was essential for the Lord's then-future crucifixion to remain hidden during the time that the gospel of the kingdom was being preached because Paul states (in I Cor. 2:7-8), that if the princes of this world had known about it, they would not have crucified the Lord, and this present dispensation never would have come to pass. Therefore, when it is read with the limited understanding which the apostles had at that time, Isaiah fifty-three is indeed a cryptic passage:

> *Isaiah 53:1-12: Who hath believed our report? and to whom is the arm of the LORD revealed? For he shall grow up before him as a tender plant, and as a root out of a dry ground: he hath no form nor comeliness; and when we shall see him, there is no beauty that we should desire him. He is despised and rejected of men; a man of sorrows, and acquainted with grief: and we hid as it were our faces from him; he was despised, and we esteemed him not. Surely he hath borne our griefs, and carried our sorrows: yet we did esteem him stricken, smitten of God, and afflicted. But he was wounded for our transgressions, he was bruised for our iniquities: the chastisement of our peace was upon him; and with his stripes we are healed. All we like sheep have gone astray; we have turned every one to his own way; and the LORD hath laid on him the iniquity of us all. He was oppressed, and he was*

afflicted, yet he opened not his mouth: he is brought as a lamb to the slaughter, and as a sheep before her shearers is dumb, so he openeth not his mouth. He was taken from prison and from judgment: and who shall declare his generation? for he was cut off out of the land of the living: for the transgression of my people was he stricken. And he made his grave with the wicked, and with the rich in his death; because he had done no violence, neither was any deceit in his mouth. Yet it pleased the LORD to bruise him; he hath put him to grief: when thou shalt make his soul an offering for sin, he shall see his seed, he shall prolong his days, and the pleasure of the LORD shall prosper in his hand. He shall see of the travail of his soul, and shall be satisfied: by his knowledge shall my righteous servant justify many; for he shall bear their iniquities. Therefore will I divide him a portion with the great, and he shall divide the spoil with the strong; because he hath poured out his soul unto death: and he was numbered with the transgressors; and he bare the sin of many, and made intercession for the transgressors.

We must remember the imperfect understanding the apostles had at the time concerning prophecies such as Isaiah fifty-three, and be careful not to read our own understanding into their actions.

We are able to see through the dark-ened glass of obscure prophetic scriptures, but that would not mean the twelve apostles understood these passages before they were fulfilled. While the apostles may have under-stood the Messiah had to die, they did not know it would be by crucifixion; and Isaiah makes no mention of the resurrection.

A number of Christians today believe that the New Testament (or the New Cove-nant) began with the birth of the Lord Jesus Christ. The Old Testament, then, is thought to end immediately after the book of Mala-chi, with the birth of Jesus in Matthew be-ginning the New Testament. The Lord, though, inspired the author of the book of Hebrews to draw the line at the death of Je-sus, and not at His birth. The author of He-brews states that a testament requires the death of the testator and is only in force after death. Therefore, the actual New Testament could not have begun with the birth of Je-sus, according to:

> *Hebrews 9:15-18: And for this cause he is the mediator of the new testa-ment, that by means of death, for the redemption of the transgressions that were under the first testament, they which are called might receive the promise of eternal inheritance. For where a testament is, there must also of necessity be the death of the testa-tor. For a testament is of force after men are dead: otherwise it is of no strength at all while the testator liveth. Whereupon neither the first testament*

was dedicated without blood.

While this may surprise many who do not take a Dispensational approach to Bible study, it is clear from this passage that the New Testament could not have begun with the birth of Christ but rather with His death. As a matter of fact, Jesus Himself stated that the New Testament was to be implemented through His blood:

> *Mark 14:23-24: And he took the cup, and when he had given thanks, he gave it to them: and they all drank of it. And he said unto them, This is my blood of the new testament, which is shed for many.*

The New Testament, then, could not have begun with the birth of the Christ Child in the manger, as so many Christians are led to believe. Instead, it is only for convenience that the Hebrew Scriptures (the "Old Testament") have been separated from the Greek Scriptures that were written after the birth of Jesus (the so-called "New Testament"). Yet this convenience has actually become a tradition that has taught great error. Thus, in order to *"rightly divide the word of truth" (II Tim. 2:15),* we must be careful to allow the inspired scriptures themselves to be our final authority.

Because the New Testament did not begin with the birth of Jesus, this example serves to illustrate the fact that man's traditions, no matter how sincere they may be, actually can lead us astray.

We must not read back into scripture that which is revealed later.

We cannot claim
Israel's promises...

The entity the Bible refers to as Israel is a nation of people, and yet they are so much more. They are God's chosen people[1], God's elect people[2], the people of God's covenants[3], a peculiar people identified by the token of circumcision.

> And ye shall circumcise the flesh of your foreskin; and it shall be a token of the covenant betwixt me and you. (Genesis 17:11)

With this covenant, the Lord required Abraham, and subsequently all Israel, to be circumcised, along with all males in his household. Circumcision was not an option; it was a requirement. The uncircumcised man was to be cut off from his people, according to:

> Genesis 17:13-14: He that is born in thy house, and he that is bought with thy money, must needs be circumcised: and my covenant shall be in your flesh for an everlasting covenant. And the uncircumcised man child whose flesh of his foreskin is not circumcised, that soul shall be cut off from his people; he hath broken my covenant.

In stark contrast, and as a product of the revelation of the mystery, Paul says:

> Galatians 6:15: For in Christ Jesus neither circumcision availeth any thing,

nor uncircumcision, but a new creature.

To partake of the Passover required circumcision:

Exodus 12:48-49: And when a stranger shall sojourn with thee, and will keep the passover to the LORD, let all his males be circumcised, and then let him come near and keep it; and he shall be as one that is born in the land: for no uncircumcised person shall eat thereof. One law shall be to him that is homeborn, and unto the stranger that sojourneth among you.

In stark contrast, as a product of the revelation of the mystery, Paul says "...*For even Christ our passover is sacrificed for us:*" (I Corinthians 5:7)

Circumcised Israel was always to maintain separation from the uncircumcised Gentiles, as Isaiah clearly stated:

Isaiah 52:1: Awake, awake; put on thy strength, O Zion; put on thy beautiful garments, O Jerusalem, the holy city: for henceforth there shall no more come into thee the uncircumcised and the unclean.

Ezekiel also states that no uncircumcised stranger shall enter the Lord's sanctuary:

Ezekiel 44:9: Thus saith the Lord GOD; No stranger, uncircumcised in heart, nor uncircumcised in flesh, shall enter into my sanctuary, of any stranger that is among the children of Israel.

In stark contract, as a product of the

revelation of the mystery, Paul says:

*Romans 10:12: For there is no differ-
ence between the Jew and the Greek:
for the same Lord over all is rich unto
all that call upon him.*

*Romans 3:22: Even the righteousness
of God which is by faith of Jesus Christ
unto all and upon all them that believe:
for there is no difference:*

*Galatians 5:1-6 Stand fast therefore in
the liberty wherewith Christ hath made
us free, and be not entangled again
with the yoke of bondage. Behold, I
Paul say unto you, that if ye be circumcised, Christ shall profit you nothing.
For I testify again to every man that is
circumcised, that he is a debtor to do
the whole law. Christ is become of no
effect unto you, whosoever of you are
justified by the law; ye are fallen from
grace. For we through the Spirit wait
for the hope of righteousness by faith.
For in Jesus Christ neither circumcision
availeth any thing, nor uncircumcision;
but faith which worketh by love.*

Spiritualizing Israel's circumcision will
not work because Israel's circumcision was
not spiritual but the actual cutting away of
physical flesh. In stark contrast, as a product of the revelation of the mystery, Paul
says:

*Colossians 2:11: In whom also ye are
circumcised with the circumcision
made without hands, in putting off the
body of the sins of the flesh by the circumcision of Christ:*

Philippians 3:3: For we are the circumcision, which worship God in the spirit, and rejoice in Christ Jesus, and have no confidence in the flesh.

In addition, the Lord had called Israel to be His chosen people from the start and severed them from other people (the Gentiles), as the Bible clearly states:

Leviticus 20:25-26: Ye shall therefore put difference between clean beasts and unclean, and between unclean fowls and clean: and ye shall not make your souls abominable by beast, or by fowl, or by any manner of living thing that creepeth on the ground, which I have separated from you as unclean. And ye shall be holy unto me: for I the LORD am holy, and have severed you from other people, that ye should be mine.

Numbers 23:9:...lo, the people shall dwell alone, and shall not be reckoned among the nations.

With the fall of Israel, and in stark contrast (as a product of the revelation of the mystery), Paul, declares that the body of Christ involves *"...every one members one of another."* (Romans 12:5)

Galatians 3:28: There is neither Jew nor Greek, there is neither bond nor free, there is neither male nor female: for ye are all one in Christ Jesus.

Understanding that we cannot claim Israel's promises is profound as it dismantles British Israelism, Aryan Supremacy, Manifest Destiny, fulfillment of prophecy in 1948 and

and many other beliefs commonly held.

How many people this very day, how many influential people in high government positions in the USA, Britain and other countries still hold to:

> Genesis 12:3: *And I will bless them that bless thee, and curse him that curseth thee: and in thee shall all families of the earth be blessed.*

This blessing was to occur initially through Abraham's descendants, which the Bible refers to as Abraham's "seed" plural, numbered "as the dust of the earth:"

> Genesis 13:14-16: *And the LORD said unto Abram, after that Lot was separated from him, Lift up now thine eyes, and look from the place where thou art northward, and southward, and eastward, and westward: For all the land which thou seest, to thee will I give it, and to thy seed for ever. And I will make thy seed as the dust of the earth: so that if a man can number the dust of the earth, then shall thy seed also be numbered.*

> Genesis 26:4: *And I will make thy seed to multiply as the stars of heaven, and will give unto thy seed all these countries; and in thy seed shall all the nations of the earth be blessed;*

Blessings upon the plural seed were extended to Abraham's progeny Isaac *(Exodus 35:12)* and Jacob *(Genesis 28:4),* whose name was changed to Israel *(Genesis 32:28);* and in each instance it is a vast number likened to *"...the dust of the earth." (Genesis 28:14)*

In stark contrast, as a product of the revelation of the mystery, Paul presents the Lord Jesus Christ as the "seed" singular, not plural.

Galatians 3:16: Now to Abraham and his seed were the promises made. He saith not, And to seeds, as of many; but as of one, And to thy seed, which is Christ.

We must not allow our English word "seed" to be a source of confusion because its singularity or plurality is always identified by the immediate context. We are not confused when we have one seed in our hand or a fifty pound bag of seed on our shoulder, for we know the word "seed" can be either singular or plural, but not both at the same time.

When God promised to bless those who blessed Abraham's seed, that promise concerned those who blessed the nation of Israel. Throughout the Old Testament (including the four gospels prior to Calvary), those Gentiles who blessed Israel received the Lord's blessing, since Israel was His chosen nation.

This explains the Lord Jesus' dealings with Gentiles in the four gospels and makes what most people find to be difficult passages very easy to understand.

Matthew 15:22-28: And, behold, a woman of Canaan came out of the same coasts, and cried unto him, saying, Have mercy on me, O Lord, thou Son of David; my daughter is griev-

ously vexed with a devil. But he answered her not a word. And his disciples came and besought him, saying, Send her away; for she crieth after us. But he answered and said, I am not sent but unto the lost sheep of the house of Israel. Then came she and worshipped him, saying, Lord, help me. [26] But he answered and said, It is not meet to take the children's bread, and to cast it to dogs. And she said, Truth, Lord: yet the dogs eat of the crumbs which fall from their masters' table. Then Jesus answered and said unto her, O woman, great is thy faith: be it unto thee even as thou wilt. And her daughter was made whole from that very hour.

One need not make excuses for the Lord's being rude; one need not set forth that the Canaanite woman was being tested; one need not tell stories about the manners and customs of the people in the first century. One need only recognize that Jesus had come to Israel and this lady was a Gentile dog. When she gave testimony that she understood Israel's exalted position and her lowly status, the Lord blessed her in accordance with the promises made to Abraham's people when they had been blessed by a Gentile.

That is exactly what goes on in *Luke 7:2-9* :

And a certain centurion's servant, who was dear unto him, was sick, and ready to die. And when he heard of Je-

sus, he sent unto him the elders of the Jews, beseeching him that he would come and heal his servant. And when they came to Jesus, they besought him instantly, saying, That he was worthy for whom he should do this: For he loveth our nation, and he hath built us a synagogue. Then Jesus went with them. And when he was now not far from the house, the centurion sent friends to him, saying unto him, Lord, trouble not thyself: for I am not worthy that thou shouldest enter under my roof: Wherefore neither thought I myself worthy to come unto thee: but say in a word, and my servant shall be healed. For I also am a man set under authority, having under me soldiers, and I say unto one, Go, and he goeth; and to another, Come, and he cometh; and to my servant, Do this, and he doeth it. When Jesus heard these things, he marvelled at him, and turned him about, and said unto the people that followed him, I say unto you, I have not found so great faith, no, not in Israel.

The Lord had committed Himself to bless them who blessed Abraham's seed (plural); and since the Centurion had built Israel a synagogue, the Centurion was a recipient of the blessing promised.

It was in this manner, then, that the Lord separated the nation of Israel and gave Israel the preeminence above all the other nations; and this continues during the earthly ministry of the Lord Jesus Christ.

In Christ Jesus we have the seed (singular) by which all people of the earth, without distinction, receive all spiritual blessings by faith in the gospel of Christ rather than by circumcision and the works of the law mandated by Israel's covenants.

Christ, in His earthly ministry "...*was a minister of the circumcision for the truth of God, to confirm the promises made unto the fathers:*" (Romans 15:8).

No Gentiles were considered "circumcision" and no Gentiles were given any promises according to Israel's covenants. Be reminded that the same people who were given the Old Testament are those who get the New Testament.[4]

At this present time, although Israel has rejected Jesus Christ as her Messiah, Christians gain no advantage in the Lord's eyes by blessing that nation, because salvation by grace alone is through the fall of Israel.

> *Romans 11:11: I say then, Have they stumbled that they should fall? God forbid: but rather through their fall salvation is come unto the Gentiles, for to provoke them to jealousy.*

Were you to receive a blessing today as a product of your having blessed Israel, that would be directly contrary to the "*...one mediator between God and men, the man Christ Jesus;*" (1 Timothy 2:5) "*For other foundation can no man lay than that is laid, which is Jesus Christ.*" (I Corinthians 3:11)

Paul would not have us to be ignorant

of the fact that we cannot claim Israel's promises:

> *Romans 11:25-28: For I would not, brethren, that ye should be ignorant of this mystery, lest ye should be wise in your own conceits; that blindness in part is happened to Israel, until the fulness of the Gentiles be come in. And so all Israel shall be saved: as it is written, There shall come out of Sion the Deliverer, and shall turn away ungodliness from Jacob: For this is my covenant unto them, when I shall take away their sins. As concerning the gospel, they are enemies for your sakes: but as touching the election, they are beloved for the fathers' sakes.*

Israel shall be saved; Israel shall be delivered: Israel will receive God's covenant promises to them. We are the Body of Christ, we are not Israel. To miss that fact is to be blinded, an enemy of the gospel of the grace of God which is not according to Israel's promise but according to the revelation of the mystery.

---

1. *Deuteronomy 7:6 For thou art an holy people unto the LORD thy God: the LORD thy God hath chosen thee to be a special people unto himself, above all people that are upon the face of the earth.*

2. *Jeremiah 45:4 Thus shalt thou say unto him, The LORD saith thus; Behold, that which I have built will I break down, and that which I have planted I will pluck up, even this whole land.*

3. Ephesians 2:12 That at that time ye were without Christ, being aliens from the commonwealth of Israel, and strangers from the covenants of promise, having no hope, and without God in the world:

4. Jeremiah 31:31 Behold, the days come, saith the LORD, that I will make a new covenant with the house of Israel, and with the house of Judah:

Hebrews 8:8 For finding fault with them, he saith, Behold, the days come, saith the Lord, when I will make a new covenant with the house of Israel and with the house of Judah:

We cannot claim Israel's Messiah or Israel's commission...

Few things in the Bible are more easily discerned than the fact that Jesus Christ was Israel's Messiah.

— It is easily discerned in prophecy:

Ezekiel 3:4-6: And he said unto me, Son of man, go, get thee unto the house of Israel, and speak with my words unto them. For thou art not sent to a people of a strange speech and of an hard language, but to the house of Israel; Not to many people of a strange speech and of an hard language, whose words thou canst not understand. Surely, had I sent thee to them, they would have hearkened unto thee.

— It is easily discerned in ministry statements made by Christ Himself:

Matthew 10:5-6: These twelve Jesus sent forth, and commanded them, saying, Go not into the way of the Gentiles, and into any city of the Samaritans enter ye not: But go rather to the lost sheep of the house of Israel.

— It is easily discerned in Paul's statement defining Christ's ministry:

Romans 15:8: Now I say that Jesus

Christ was a minister of the circumcision for the truth of God, to confirm the promises made unto the fathers:
While we can recall the account of the Canaanite woman (a Gentile) who asked Christ to heal her daughter who was *"grievously vexed with a devil,"* we should remind ourselves here that the Lord initially refused to honor her request.[1] Only after the Gentile woman acknowledged her own inferior position as a Gentile, thus effectively blessing the nation of Israel (the seed of Abraham), did He agree to heal her daughter in accordance with God's promise to Gentiles through Abraham.[2]

Jesus did not bless the Canaanite woman and heal her daughter because the dispensation of grace had begun, but rather because it hadn't. There is neither Jew nor Greek, *(Galatians 3:28)* in this present dispensation, which means that what took place in Matthew fifteen could not happen now.
"He came unto his own, and his own received him not." *(John 1:11);* and while there were exceptions that did accept Christ as Israel's Messiah, the exceptions prove the rule.
The Old Testament belonged to Israel; and we know from the book of Hebrews that the four gospel accounts prior to the cross are Old Testament in their doctrine.[3]
The four gospels record the prophesied rise of Israel into its earthly kingdom status; yet we know that Gentile salvation comes as

a product of Israel's fall.[4]

These things being true, one might ask, "How could this happen? How could such obvious truth be missed?" The answer is found in church history: for more than 1000 years very few people had access to a Bible, and fewer yet read from Paul. David Daniell in <u>The Bible In English</u> says, "A neat definition of the Reformation is 'People reading Paul.'"

Whatever the reason, the Christian church long has been centered and focused upon the four gospels; and the difficulties encountered in getting right division right are exacerbated by what happens immediately after the resurrection of the Lord.

Rather than a new dispensation according to the revelation of the mystery, after the cross the law continues and the separation between Gentile and Israel is maintained.

Instead of the second chapter of Acts being the birthday of a new church it is actually the near death experience of old Israel.

Peter recounted the promise Christ had made to Israel *"For John truly baptized with water; but ye shall be baptized with the Holy Ghost not many days hence." (Acts 1:5).* It is the fruition of that promise to Israel that took place at Pentecost, and not the start of something new.

The audience at Pentecost is identified clearly in Acts chapter two as being *"...Jews, devout men, out of every nation "(v5), "Ye men of Judaea" (v14), "Ye men of Israel" (v22), "all the house of Israel "(v36).*

Even *"them that are far off" (v39)* would be people of Israel who did not make it to town for the feast of Pentecost.

Further, Gentiles were not a part of Israel's feast program nor were they included in the prophecy dealing with this event:

Ezekiel 36:24-28: For I will take you from among the heathen, and gather you out of all countries, and will bring you into your own land. Then will I sprinkle clean water upon you, and ye shall be clean: from all your filthiness, and from all your idols, will I cleanse you. A new heart also will I give you, and a new spirit will I put within you: and I will take away the stony heart out of your flesh, and I will give you an heart of flesh. And I will put my spirit within you, and cause you to walk in my statutes, and ye shall keep my judgments, and do them. And ye shall dwell in the land that I gave to your fathers; and ye shall be my people, and I will be your God.

Peter also stated that what Luke reported in Acts chapter two is about Israel's *"last days" (Acts 2:17)* because *"...this is that which was spoken by the prophet Joel;" (Acts 2:16)*; and anything from prophecy could hardly be *"...according to the revelation of the mystery, which was kept secret since the world began," (Romans 16:25)*

To include Gentiles or to misidentify the early chapters in the book of Acts as the Body of Christ is difficult because Peter preached doctrine appropriate to *"...the time of Jacob's trouble,"* (Jeremiah 30:7)

The Holy Ghost comfort was promised to Israel and it was to Israel that Peter spoke. We can be certain of that fact because eight chapters later in the book of Acts, Peter *"...said unto them, Ye know how that it is an unlawful thing for a man that is a Jew to keep company, or come unto one of another nation; but God hath shewed me that I should not call any man common or unclean."* (Acts 10:28). Peter could not have included Gentiles in Acts chapter two when it was not until Acts chapter ten that Peter began to learn that things were changing.

The *"them that are far off"* (Acts 2:39) are well described in *Daniel 9:7"...to the men of Judah, and to the inhabitants of Jerusalem, and unto all Israel, that are near, and that are far off..."*

Chronologically, between the four gospels (which many wrongly believe to be the Christian pattern) and the early chapters of the book of Acts (which many wrongly believe to be the birthday of our church today) are situated the verses which most people wrongly believe to be our marching orders: the so-called "Great Commission."

Firstly, the Lord gave a pre-crucifixion commission which is very different in content to the post-resurrection commission:

Matthew 10:5-7: These twelve Jesus sent forth, and commanded them, saying, Go not into the way of the Gentiles, and into any city of the Samari-

tans enter ye not: But go rather to the lost sheep of the house of Israel. And as ye go, preach, saying, The kingdom of heaven is at hand.

Note that the Lord sent His disciples to all nations in the post-resurrection commission:

Matthew 28:19-20:   Go ye therefore, and teach all nations, baptizing them in the name of the Father, and of the Son, and of the Holy Ghost: Teaching them to observe all things whatsoever I have commanded you: and, lo, I am with you alway, even unto the end of the world.

The confusion is removed when we remember that the apostles themselves did not go to all nations as the verses in Matthew twenty-eight required because they could not.   They knew certain things had to take place first.

The end had to come:

— *Matthew 24:14: And this gospel of the kingdom shall be preached in all the world for a witness unto all nations; and then shall the end come.*

The kingdom promised to Israel needed to be restored:

— *Isaiah 52:1: Awake, awake; put on thy strength, O Zion; put on thy beautiful garments, O Jerusalem, the holy city: for henceforth there shall no more come into thee the uncircumcised and the unclean.*

— *Ezekiel 44:9:   Thus saith the Lord God; No stranger, uncircumcised in heart, nor uncircumcised in flesh, shall enter into my sanctuary, of any stranger that is among the children of Israel.*

The apostles, knowing that the prophesied sanctification of Gentiles must occur through the exaltation of Israel, had no reason to go directly to "all nations" in the "Great Commission." Instead, they expected the kingdom to first be "restored again to Israel", as their own words reflect:

Acts1:6-8: When they therefore were come together, they asked of him, saying, Lord, wilt thou at this time restore again the kingdom to Israel? And he said unto them, It is not for you to know the times or the seasons, which the Father hath put in his own power. But ye shall receive power, after that the Holy Ghost is come upon you: and ye shall be witnesses unto me both in Jerusalem, and in all Judaea, and in Samaria, and unto the uttermost part of the earth.

The apostles' question in verse six demonstrates their understanding that the prophesied kingdom must first be established before the Gentiles could be made acceptable to the Lord. Because Israel was not being exalted, the apostles were clearly confined in their ministries to the nation Israel alone. [6]

Before dealing with uncircumcised Gentiles, the apostles would first need to convert unbelieving Israel in preparation for Israel's kingdom:

Luke 24:47: And that repentance and remission of sins should be preached in his name among all nations, beginning at Jerusalem.

Notice the verse says "among" all nations, not to all nations, and as late as Acts 21:20 believing Israel rejoiced in *"...how many thousands of Jews there are which believe; and they are all zealous of the law:"*

Zealous of the law, not grateful for grace through faith.

Since the prophesied kingdom had not yet been established, the apostles continued to confine their ministry to Israel alone, fully expecting the Jews to repent. The reality was that the prophesied kingdom with Israel at the head of the nations had yet to appear, and it wasn't going to.

Deuteronomy 28:10-13: And all people of the earth shall see that thou art called by the name of the Lord; and they shall be afraid of thee. And the Lord shall make thee plenteous in goods, in the fruit of thy body, and in the fruit of thy cattle, and in the fruit of thy ground, in the land which the Lord sware unto thy fathers to give thee. The Lord shall open unto thee his good treasure, the heaven to give the rain unto thy land in his season, and to bless all the work of thine hand: and thou shalt lend unto many nations, and thou shalt not borrow. And the Lord shall make thee the head, and not the tail; and thou shalt be above only, and thou shalt not be beneath; if that thou hearken unto the commandments of the Lord thy God, which I command thee this day, to observe and to do them:

The apostles knew the so-called "Great Commission" required the rise of Israel; yet what they were witnessing was Israel's fall.

The Lord stopped the prophetic clock due to Israel's unbelief, and the Lord took away Israel's status and standing when Israel was declared to be *"...stiffnecked and uncircumcised in heart and ears, ye do always resist the Holy Ghost: as your fathers did, so do ye." (Acts 7:51)*

The apostles expected prophetic fulfillment of passages such as:

Zechariah 8:20-23:   Thus saith the LORD of hosts; It shall yet come to pass, that there shall come people, and the inhabitants of many cities: And the inhabitants of one city shall go to another, saying, Let us go speedily to pray before the LORD, and to seek the LORD of hosts: I will go also. Yea, many people and strong nations shall come to seek the LORD of hosts in Jerusalem, and to pray before the LORD. Thus saith the LORD of hosts; In those days it shall come to pass, that ten men shall take hold out of all languages of the nations, even shall take hold of the skirt of him that is a Jew, saying, We will go with you: for we have heard that God is with you.

What the apostles got instead of exaltation was persecution and scattering:

Acts 8:1: And Saul was consenting unto his death. And at that time there was a great persecution against the church which was at Jerusalem; and they were all scattered abroad throughout the regions of Judaea and Samaria, except the apostles.

In the very next chapter, Paul is saved and given the revelation of the mystery by the risen Lord, with a promise of additional mystery information to follow:

Acts 26:16-17: But rise, and stand upon thy feet: for I have appeared unto thee for this purpose, to make thee a minister and a witness both of these things which thou hast seen, and of those things in the which I will appear unto thee; Delivering thee from the people, and from the Gentiles, unto whom now I send thee:

With the revelation of the mystery, the very men to whom the "Great Commission" was given rescinded those instructions because of the new information that had been given to Paul.

Galatians 2:7-9: But contrariwise, when they saw that the gospel of the uncircumcision was committed unto me, as the gospel of the circumcision was unto Peter; (For he that wrought effectually in Peter to the apostleship of the circumcision, the same was mighty in me toward the Gentiles:) And when James, Cephas, and John, who seemed to be pillars, perceived the grace that was given unto me, they gave to me and Barnabas the right hands of fellowship; that we should go unto the heathen, and they unto the circumcision.

How very simple it is to see that Peter, in possession of the keys of the kingdom with binding and loosing power,[7] bound on earth and in heaven that the "Great Commission" was no longer operative. At that point, Israel's apostles had no intention of going to every nation and all creatures, but to the circumcision only. This agreement, borne witness to in Acts chapter fifteen, has escaped the attention of churches for nearly two thousand years.

Just as certainly as the prophecy from Joel with respect to the sun and moon, which Peter properly repeated at Pentecost, did not come to pass, just that certainly the "Great Commission" was set aside by the men to whom the Lord Himself gave that authority.

Acts 2:16,19-20 But this is that which was spoken by the prophet Joel;...I will shew wonders in heaven above, and signs in the earth beneath; blood, and fire, and vapour of smoke: The sun shall be turned into darkness, and the moon into blood, before that great and notable day of the Lord come:

By the inspiration of the Holy Ghost, Peter correctly said "*...this is that which was spoken by the prophet Joel;*" (Acts 2:16). The fact that the items prophesied did not happen at that time declares the interruption of the prophetic program with that which

Paul was to identify as the revelation of the mystery.

The apostles did not see *"...the abomination of desolation, spoken of by Daniel the prophet, stand in the holy place," (Matthew 24:15)*

With the cessation of prophetic fulfillment and with the Lord's saving uncircumcised Gentiles without the works of the law,[8] the apostles confined their activities to those that constituted believing Israel, just as they agreed to do in Galatians chapter two.[9]

There was a new message, a new messenger and a new pattern: all of which are easily discerned in the verses which remain a mystery to most people who call themselves "Christians."

> *Ephesians 3:2: If ye have heard of the dispensation of the grace of God which is given me to youward:*
>
> *1 Timothy 1:16: Howbeit for this cause I obtained mercy, that in me first Jesus Christ might shew forth all long-suffering, for a pattern to them which should hereafter believe on him to life everlasting.*
>
> *Romans 11:13: For I speak to you Gentiles, inasmuch as I am the apostle of the Gentiles, I magnify mine office:*

All of the prophecies concerning the kingdom will be fulfilled; but their fulfillment has been postponed.

For these many reasons, it clearly is wrong for members of the body of Christ according to the revelation of the mystery to claim Israel's Messiah or Israel's commissions.

The Lord has a greater commission for us, a grace commission:

II Corinthians 5:19-20: To wit, that God was in Christ, reconciling the world unto himself, not imputing their trespasses unto them; and hath committed unto us the word of reconciliation. Now then we are ambassadors for Christ, as though God did beseech you by us: we pray you in Christ's stead, be ye reconciled to God.

---

1. *Matthew 15:22-28 And, behold, a woman of Canaan came out of the same coasts, and cried unto him, saying, Have mercy on me, O Lord, thou son of David; my daughter is grievously vexed with a devil. But he answered her not a word. And his disciples came and besought him, saying, Send her away; for she crieth after us. But he answered and said, I am not sent but unto the lost sheep of the house of Israel. Then came she and worshipped him, saying, Lord, help me. But he answered and said, It is not meet to take the children's bread, and to cast it to dogs. And she said, Truth, Lord: yet the dogs eat of the crumbs which fall from their masters' table. Then Jesus answered and said unto her, O woman, great is thy faith: be it unto thee even as thou wilt. And her daughter was made whole from that very hour.*

2. *Genesis 12:3 And I will bless them that bless thee, and curse him that curseth thee: and in thee shall all families of the earth be blessed.*

3. *Hebrews 9:15-18 And for this cause he is the mediator of the new testament, that by means of death, for the redemption of the transgressions that were under the first testament, they which are called might receive the promise of eternal inheritance. For where a testament is, there must also of necessity be the death of the testator. For a testament is of force after men are dead: otherwise it is of no strength at all while the testator liveth. Whereupon neither the first testament was dedicated without blood.*

4. *Romans 11:11 I say then, Have they stumbled that they should fall? God forbid: but rather through their fall salvation is come unto the Gentiles, for to provoke them to jealousy.*

5. *The Bible In English*, David Daniell, Yale University Press, pg 10.

6. It is also illuminating to note the contradiction between Matthew 24:14 and Colossians 1:23 as mentioned earlier.

7. Matthew 16:19 *And I will give unto thee the keys of the kingdom of heaven: and whatsoever thou shalt bind on earth shall be bound in heaven: and whatsoever thou shalt loose on earth shall be loosed in heaven.*

8. Acts 13:38 *Be it known unto you therefore, men and brethren, that through this man is preached unto you the forgiveness of sins: And by him all that believe are justified from all things, from which ye could not be justified by the law of Moses.*

9. Galatians 2:9 *And when James, Cephas, and John, who seemed to be pillars, perceived the grace that was given unto me, they gave to me and Barnabas the right hands of fellowship; that we should go unto the heathen, and they unto the circumcision.*

We cannot rob Israel of its New Testament

It is obvious that the Old Testament belonged to Israel, and it is just as obvious that the New Testament also belongs to Israel. There can be neither doubt nor confusion about those two facts.[1]

If those were the only two choices, Old versus New Testament, it would not be difficult to understand why most everyone would conclude they were that described as the "New." And most people have never considered a third choice, a new creature, the church the body of Christ, put in place as a result of the revelation of the mystery given to Paul.

The multitudes who know only the two choices, Old versus New Testament, of necessity, conclude that they are the recipients of Israel's covenant promises, old or new. Some teach that today's church replaced Israel, some assert that we have become spiritual Israel, some say that God's physical promises were for Old Israel and we are New Israel and get the spiritual promises, and some actually claim to be literal physical Israel. All are wrong and they all have missed the revelation of the mystery.

Part of the reason it is so easy to miss the mystery is that so little attention is called to it, while every Bible ever printed emphasizes the existence of the Old and New Testaments.

What if you purchased a Bible that had Paul's thirteen books printed on a light pastel robin's egg blue paper with dark blue type? With just that simple device, Paul's writings would call themselves to your attention. Similarly, the fact that Jesus' words are printed in red in most Bibles calls attention to them when every word in the Bible is the word of God; and more importantly, the doctrinal truth is that Christ's words in the red letters are not even spoken to us.

We already noted that the first sixty-nine chapters of the Bible are not Old Testament and we already noted that the chapters in Matthew, Mark, Luke and John before the crucifixion are Old Testament and not New. What we need to learn is that there is a third choice, neither Old nor New Testament, but mystery truth revealed about the body of Christ, in which there is neither Jew nor Greek: hence neither Old nor New.

In the four gospels, the Lord Jesus never informed the apostles that uncircumcised Gentiles ever would be cleansed. Nor was the sanctification of uncircumcised Gentiles the subject of any prophecy. Instead, even during the early portion of the book of Acts, Peter's understanding was that only Israel would receive the Lord's blessing directly, and that the nations of the earth would be blessed through Israel's exaltation.

After the cross, after Pentecost, Peter maintained that Gentiles were to be blessed through the rise of Israel according to Israel's covenants:

Acts 3:25: Ye are the children of the prophets, and of the covenant which God made with our fathers, saying unto Abraham, And in thy seed shall all the kindreds of the earth be blessed.

And so Peter, with the keys of the kingdom in hand and the Holy Ghost upon him had not moved an inch from:

Genesis 26:4: And I will make thy seed to multiply as the stars of heaven, and will give unto thy seed all these countries; and in thy seed shall all the nations of the earth be blessed;

Genesis 28:14: And thy seed shall be as the dust of the earth, and thou shalt spread abroad to the west, and to the east, and to the north, and to the south: and in thee and in thy seed shall all the families of the earth be blessed.

Peter continued to preach the seed (plural) nation Israel, not knowing of the seed (singular), *"...He saith not, And to seeds, as of many; but as of one, And to thy seed, which is Christ., (Galatians 3:16)*, which is Christ according to the revelation of the mystery.

Since Peter would have nothing to do with a Gentile as late as Acts chapter ten, for people and denominations to put Gentiles in Acts chapter two is intellectually dishonest:

Acts 10:28: And he said unto them, Ye know how that it is an unlawful thing for a man that is a Jew to keep company, or come unto one of another nation; ...

Then neither were uncircumcised Gentiles to be included in any of his other early Acts sermons. In fact, Peter's understanding that Christ was a Saviour only to Israel also is reflected by his answer to the Jewish high priest:

> *Acts 5:30-31: The God of our fathers raised up Jesus, whom ye slew and hanged on a tree. Him hath God exalted with his right hand to be a Prince and a Saviour, for to give repentance to Israel, ...*

What this means is that after the cross, Israel's New Testament could begin, and so it had. What we read in each of the four gospels and in the early part of the book of Acts is still about Israel and Israel's kingdom, with Gentiles still as outcasts unless they proselytize into the nation Israel.

And proselytize into the nation Israel was what Cornelius did in Acts chapter ten.

It was in the tenth chapter of Acts that the Lord sent Peter a vision of a great sheet let down to the earth, filled with unclean beasts, in order to prepare Peter for his encounter with uncircumcised Gentiles. Peter, though, initially refused these unclean beasts:

> *Acts10:10-15: And he became very hungry, and would have eaten: but while they made ready, he fell into a trance, And saw heaven opened, and a certain vessel descending unto him, as it had been a great sheet knit at the four corners, and let down to the earth: Wherein were all manner of fourfooted beasts of the earth, and wild beasts,*

and creeping things, and fowls of the air. And there came a voice to him, Rise, Peter; kill, and eat. But Peter said, Not so, Lord; for I have never eaten any thing that is common or unclean. And the voice spake unto him again the second time, What God hath cleansed, that call not thou common.

Up to this point, Peter and the other apostles had continued keeping the Law, having never been taught otherwise. In the vision, the Gentiles were represented by the unclean beasts, and the Law forbade the Jews from eating unclean beasts.[2]

Although Cornelius feared God and gave alms to the nation of Israel, he was still an uncircumcised Gentile. Since the Jews were required to remain separate from "the nations," Peter therefore considered all uncircumcised men such as Cornelius to be unclean until the Lord Himself made it clear that they had been cleansed and could join with Peter.

Acts10:28: And he said unto them, Ye know how that it is an unlawful thing for a man that is a Jew to keep company, or come unto one of another nation; but God hath shewed me that I should not call any man common or unclean.

Peter came to this realization when Cornelius spoke in tongues: since tongues were signs for unbelieving Jews,[3] Peter was the unbelieving Jew who learned Cornelius was acceptable by the sign of tongues.

In understanding this, we are then able

to gain even more clarity when we realize that Peter made no mention of Paul or Paul's gospel of the grace of God in dealing with Cornelius.

Cornelius, like the Canaanite woman and the Roman Centurion, was blessed because he had blessed the nation Israel. Cornelius was not blessed by Israel's fall, which means that Cornelius is not a pattern of Gentile salvation into the body of Christ today.

Peter would stay with his kingdom message for Israel, knowing to welcome Gentiles such as Cornelius. Paul would stay with his message of grace salvation to Israel and Gentiles without distinction. Peter and Paul would separate and go their own ways:[4] national Israel was declared fallen and Paul's message continues to this very day, with people still saying "You robbed Peter to pay Paul." When Peter and his followers died, any hope for Israel (temporarily) died with them.

Some confusion is engendered in Acts chapter six when the "Grecians" are mentioned for the first time. Although it would be natural to assume that the Grecians were Gentiles, it would be wrong.

We have seen, based upon Acts chapter ten and Cornelius, that Peter could not have been preaching to Gentiles at Pentecost. This also would be true for the sixth chapter of Acts; and all we know from the fact that these people are called Grecians is that they were from Greece.

Even as late as Acts chapter eleven, the disciples (who were "scattered abroad" after

Stephen was stoned in Acts chapter seven) were still preaching the word to the Jews only:

> *Acts 11:19: Now they which were scattered abroad upon the persecution that arose about Stephen travelled as far as Phenice, and Cyprus, and Antioch, preaching the word to none but unto the Jews only.*

What all this shows is that after the cross, including Pentecost and the early Acts period, we read about the kingdom actually being offered to Israel for the first time. While the kingdom was the focus of the four gospels, the kingdom could not be offered until the sacrifice of the Messiah had taken place.[5]

We cannot rob Israel of these New Testament chapters which follow the cross. We can, however, recognize that national Israel fails and falls:

> *Acts 7:51: Ye stiffnecked and uncircumcised in heart and ears, ye do always resist the Holy Ghost: as your fathers did, so do ye.*
>
> *Romans 11:26-28: And so all Israel shall be saved: as it is written, There shall come out of Sion the Deliverer, and shall turn away ungodliness from Jacob: For this is my covenant unto them, when I shall take away their sins. As concerning the gospel, they are enemies for your sakes: but as touching the election, they are beloved for the fathers' sakes.*

And so Israel's national salvation is yet

future and will occur when Christ returns as their Deliverer. The New Testament covenants are still for them, not for us.

Mixing Peter with Paul and confusing their separate and different messages is to rob Israel of its New Testament; and we will not do that because we have learned to rightly divide the word of truth.

---

1. *Jeremiah 31:31-33 Behold, the days come, saith the LORD, that I will make a new covenant with the house of Israel, and with the house of Judah: Not according to the covenant that I made with their fathers in the day that I took them by the hand to bring them out of the land of Egypt; which my covenant they brake, although I was an husband unto them, saith the LORD: But this shall be the covenant that I will make with the house of Israel; After those days, saith the LORD, I will put my law in their inward parts, and write it in their hearts; and will be their God, and they shall be my people.*

Hebrews 8:8-10 For finding fault with them, he saith, Behold, the days come, saith the Lord, when I will make a new covenant with the house of Israel and with the house of Judah: Not according to the covenant that I made with their fathers in the day when I took them by the hand to lead them out of the land of Egypt; because they continued not in my covenant, and I regarded them not, saith the Lord. For this is the covenant that I will make with the house of Israel after those days, saith the Lord; I will put my laws into their mind, and write them in their hearts: and I will be to them a God, and they shall be to me a people:

2. *Leviticus 11:2 Speak unto the children of Israel, saying, These are the beasts which ye shall eat among all the beasts that are on the earth.*

Leviticus 11:4 Nevertheless these shall ye not eat of them that chew the cud, or of them that divide the hoof: as the camel, because he cheweth the cud, but divideth not the hoof; he is unclean unto you.

3. *1 Corinthians 14:22 Wherefore tongues are for a sign, not to them that believe, but to them that believe not: but prophesying serveth not for them that believe not, but for them which believe.*

I Corinthians 1:22 For the Jews require a sign, and the Greeks seek after wisdom:

4. *Galatians 2:9 And when James, Cephas, and John, who seemed to be pillars, perceived the grace that was given unto me, they gave to me and Barnabas the right hands of fellowship; that we should go unto the heathen, and they unto the circumcision.*

5. *Matthew 26:28 For this is my blood of the new testament, which is shed for many for the remission of sins.*

We must recognize that the Prophecy Program has been interrupted

It is common in malls and large hotels and theme parks to have a map kiosk with an arrow or an "x" which declares "You Are Here." Suppose some pranksters were to sneak in after closing and move every map to a wrong location so that when you read "You Are Here" you never were there? You might be a very long time getting to where you needed to be.

Good directions work to our great advantage, but woe unto us when the directions are wrong.

We were misdirected when we purchased a Bible in that only the Old and New Testaments were identified, and misidentified at that. As we have noted already, the Old Testament does not begin until sixty-nine chapters past where the Bible marks it off at the beginning of Genesis. Similarly, the New Testament cannot begin until the death of the Lord Jesus Christ; and so we are misled in these most rudimentary elements.

We also are misdirected by having the Lord's earthly ministry to Israel printed in red letters, emphasizing one portion of God's word over another by the color of the ink rather than by the shades of the doctrine.

We were misdirected when we were taught to memorize the books of the Old Testament, putting it in our minds that the four gospels are New Testament in doctrine when they are not. Compounding the confusion, we then memorized the twenty-seven books of the New Testament giving no regard whatsoever to the Pauline revelation of the mystery.

And it turns out that the most important thing we can get right in our Bible study is to distinguish the differences between and the separation of the prophecy and mystery programs found in scripture.

The Bible clearly declares the presence of mystery information made known to Paul, information which was unknown before Christ imparted it to the apostle to the Gentiles.

> *Romans 16:25: Now to him that is of power to stablish you according to my gospel, and the preaching of Jesus Christ, **according to the revelation of the mystery, which was kept secret since the world began,***
> *Ephesians 3:2-3: If ye have heard of the dispensation of the grace of God which is given me to youward: [3] How that by revelation he made known unto me the mystery; (as I wrote afore in few words,*
> *Colossians 1:26: **Even the mystery which hath been hid from ages and from generations,** but now is made manifest to his saints:*

Since the Pauline mystery had been kept secret, it then would be wrong to think that it is the same as the mysteries of the kingdom, which were composed of information which the Lord taught messianic believers in parables:

Matthew 13:11: He answered and said unto them, Because it is given unto you to know the mysteries of the kingdom of heaven, but to them it is not given.

It was no mystery that the Lord some day would scatter the children of Israel, due to their disobedience and unbelief. Nor was it a mystery that God temporarily would forsake the nation of Israel, prior to the establishment of His prophesied kingdom. Indeed, the Lord's temporary forsaking of Israel was clearly prophesied:

Isaiah 54:6-8: For the LORD hath called thee as a woman forsaken and grieved in spirit, and a wife of youth, when thou wast refused, saith thy God. For a small moment have I forsaken thee; but with great mercies will I gather thee. In a little wrath I hid my face from thee for a moment; but with everlasting kindness will I have mercy on thee, saith the LORD thy Redeemer.

The interruption of the promises of prophecy is obvious and affirmed by Jesus Christ during His earthly ministry as the Lord read:

Isaiah 61:1-2: The Spirit of the Lord GOD is upon me; because the LORD hath anointed me to preach good tidings unto the meek; he hath sent me to bind up the brokenhearted, to proclaim liberty to the captives, and the opening of the prison to them that are bound; To proclaim the acceptable year of the LORD, and the day of vengeance of our God; to comfort all that mourn;

The Lord Jesus Christ, being the author of dispensationalism, did not read the two verses in their entirety. Rather, the Lord stopped and closed the book without reading about the day of vengeance. As Isaiah wrote those two verses, there is no provision for the revelation of the mystery and the imposition of what has been nearly 2000 years of the unprophesied dispensation of the grace of God. When the Lord Jesus read those same verses, clearly He knew the revelation of the mystery was soon to come (although Christ Himself did not declare it during His earthly ministry).

Luke 4:16-21: And he came to Nazareth, where he had been brought up: and, as his custom was, he went into the synagogue on the sabbath day, and stood up for to read. And there was delivered unto him the book of the prophet Esaias. And when he had opened the book, he found the place where it was written, The Spirit of the Lord is upon me, because he hath anointed me to preach the gospel to the poor; he hath sent me to heal the brokenhearted, to preach deliverance to the captives, and recovering of sight to the blind, to set at liberty them that are bruised, To preach the acceptable year of the Lord. And he closed the book, and he gave it again to the minister, and sat down. And the eyes of all them that were in the synagogue were fastened on him. And he began to say unto them, This day is this scripture fulfilled in your ears.

The Lord closed the book and did not read about the prophecies which were not going to happen at that time. Since Christ knew the end from the beginning, He knew the revelation of the mystery was going to interrupt the prophetic program; and He expects us to understand that as well.

Another example demonstrating the interruption of the prophetic program by the revelation of the mystery happened on the day of Pentecost. Peter quoted Joel's prophecy:

Acts 2:16-21: But this is that which was spoken by the prophet Joel; And it shall come to pass in the last days, saith God, I will pour out of my Spirit upon all flesh: and your sons and your daughters shall prophesy, and your young men shall see visions, and your old men shall dream dreams: And on my servants and on my handmaidens I will pour out in those days of my Spirit; and they shall prophesy: And I will shew wonders in heaven above, and signs in the earth beneath; blood, and fire, and vapour of smoke: The sun shall be turned into darkness, and the moon into blood, before that great and notable day of the Lord come: And it shall come to pass, that whosoever shall call on the name of the Lord shall be saved.

Under the Pentecostal power and anointing of the Holy Ghost, Peter preached Joel's prophecy for Israel's time of tribulation; but most of what Peter preached did not all happen: the prophetic program was interrupted.

Joel 2:28-31: And it shall come to pass afterward, that I will pour out my spirit upon all flesh; and your sons and your daughters shall prophesy, your old men shall dream dreams, your young men shall see visions: And also upon the servants and upon the handmaids in those days will I pour out my spirit. And I will shew wonders in the heavens and in the earth, blood, and fire, and pillars of smoke. The sun shall be turned into darkness, and the moon into blood, before the great and the terrible day of the LORD come.

The prophecy program was interrupted before the sun was turned into darkness and the moon into blood. The Lord Jesus Christ Himself did the interrupting when Christ revealed the mystery to our apostle, Paul.

Ephesians 3:2, 3, 5: If ye have heard of the dispensation of the grace of God which is given me to youward: How that by revelation he made known unto me the mystery; ... Which in other ages was not made known unto the sons of men, as it is now revealed unto his holy apostles and prophets by the Spirit;

Examples abound: it is clear that the prophetic program was to be interrupted. The Lord taught that there would be a delay in many of His parables. Daniel's prophecy in chapter nine awaits the confirmation of the covenant. There are no apostles seated upon any thrones anywhere ruling and reigning with Christ. There is no peace in Jerusalem or anywhere else much.

Rather than the completion of the prophetic program, there has been an interruption for the dispensation of grace, a time during which no prophecy is being fulfilled, but rather a mystery is being revealed.

Clearly, prophecy has been interrupted by the revelation of the mystery, and, "You Are Here" in this, the dispensation of God's grace.

Rather than pranksters changing the signs, we were misdirected by churches, denominations and other Christians. Most churches teach and preach as if the mystery had not been revealed. Most Christians think they are Israel (spiritual, physical or replacement) rather than the new creature, the body of Christ. If that weren't enough, we have noted that the very manner in which Bibles are printed is misleading.

We must recognize that prophecy has been interrupted by the dispensation of the revelation of the mystery.

The Most Important truth we must learn: Prophecy vs. Mystery

Every endeavor, every hobby, every occupation has certain skill sets, certain requirements, certain parameters. That said, were you to ask "What is the most important thing I need to know?" you would probably get an answer; but you could ask that same question of several people and probably get several different answers, depending upon whom you might have asked.

If you asked a meat cutter in a grocery store, "What is the most important thing I need to know to be a butcher?" the novice might quickly say "Don't cut yourself." The apprentice might offer "Wear warm clothing because it is always cold in here." The seasoned professional might tell you "Where you put your knife determines the value and price of whatever you cut; so think about what the customer wants with every move you make." All three gave correct answers; but the one you want working for you, the one you want training others, is the seasoned pro.

Ask "What is the most important thing I need to know about Bible study?" and you will get lots of right answers, but once again you would be wise to hear the seasoned professional.

The apostle Paul says for our learning and service to be approved of God, we must *"rightly divide the word of truth."* *(II Timothy 2:15)* That is not the answer you would get from a novice nor even an apprentice, and sadly, not even from many who have been around for a long time; but age and acumen do not always go hand-in-hand.

Rightly dividing the difference(s) between the Mystery and the Prophecy programs is the most important thing a Bible student can learn, but just making that statement is insufficient of itself. Here is proof.

We must learn to recognize that there are two separate and distinct bodies of information in the Bible, separate programs identified as Prophecy and Mystery.

That which is described as the Prophecy program is that which was spoken by the mouth of all the prophets, since the world began.

> *Luke 1:70: As he spake by the mouth of his holy prophets, which have been since the world began:*
> *Acts 3:21: Whom the heaven must receive until the times of restitution of all things, which God hath spoken by the mouth of all his holy prophets since the world began.*

Separate and apart from what all the prophets spoke since the world began is the Mystery information which none of the prophets spoke because the Mystery had been hidden since the world began.

Romans 16:25-26: Now to him that is of power to stablish you according to my gospel, and the preaching of Jesus Christ, according to the revelation of the mystery, which was kept secret since the world began, But now is made manifest, and by the scriptures of the prophets, according to the commandment of the everlasting God, made known to all nations for the obedience of faith:

Ephesians 3:9: And to make all men see what is the fellowship of the mystery, which from the beginning of the world hath been hid in God, who created all things by Jesus Christ:

Clearly, that data which was spoken by all would have to be different and excluded from that data which was known by none.

Most people have heard of the Old and New Testaments, but both of those were spoken of by the mouth of all the holy prophets; and so both the Old and New Testaments must be included in the Prophecy program.

Jeremiah 31:31: Behold, the days come, saith the LORD, that I will make a new covenant with the house of Israel, and with the house of Judah:

Hebrews 8:8: For finding fault with them, he saith, Behold, the days come, saith the Lord, when I will make a new covenant with the house of Israel and with the house of Judah:

The Prophecy program is centered

upon the Old Testament people Israel receiving their kingdom on this Earth under the King of Kings.

> *Revelation 11:15: And the seventh angel sounded; and there were great voices in heaven, saying, The kingdoms of this world are become the kingdoms of our Lord, and of his Christ; and he shall reign for ever and ever.*

Unknown to the people of the Prophecy program was that God would reveal a Mystery by which God would create a new celestial[1] creature to operate in heavenly places[2] for His glory.

While most everyone recognizes the existence of both the Old and New Testaments, hardly any recognize the presence of a third element, the Mystery. This is perplexing since the Bible plainly declares that we are to make the mystery known, we are to preach Christ according to the revelation of the mystery, and we are to be faithful stewards of the mystery doctrines.

> *Ephesians 3:9: And to make all men see what is the fellowship of the mystery, which from the beginning of the world hath been hid in God, who created all things by Jesus Christ:*
>
> *Romans 16:25: Now to him that is of power to stablish you according to my gospel, and the preaching of Jesus Christ, according to the revelation of the mystery, which was kept secret since the world began,*
>
> *I Corinthians 4:1: Let a man so account of us, as of the ministers of Christ, and*

stewards of the mysteries of God.

Not only have most people missed the Mystery, most have put on spiritual blinders by identifying themselves as "New Testament Christians," a term which does not exist in the Bible and actually constitutes an oxymoron.

Matthew, Mark, Luke and John contain much of the information by which these "New Testament Christians" strive to pattern themselves, apparently not knowing that they are actually attempting to conform with Old Testament Israel.

> *Hebrews 9:16-17: For where a testament is, there must also of necessity be the death of the testator. For a testament is of force after men are dead: otherwise it is of no strength at all while the testator liveth.*

Because of this, these "New Testament Christians" often pray "for the furtherance of Thy kingdom" even though that kingdom was promised to Israel and is the centerpiece of the Prophecy program.

> *Matthew 25:34: Then shall the King say unto them on his right hand, Come, ye blessed of my Father, inherit the kingdom prepared for you from the foundation of the world:*

Noting that the kingdom was prepared "from the foundation of the world," we cannot help but note the similarity to the Prophecy program and how it was spoken of by all the prophets "since the world began."

The Mystery information was kept hidden since the world began; so it can only be that it was kept secret and involves neither the Old nor the New Testaments.

I Corinthians 2:7: But we speak the wisdom of God in a mystery, even the hidden wisdom, which God ordained before the world unto our glory:

II Timothy 1:9: Who hath saved us, and called us with an holy calling, not according to our works, but according to his own purpose and grace, which was given us in Christ Jesus before the world began,

Few things could be more different than rising to one's feet as opposed to falling to the floor, and the difference between Prophecy and Mystery is equally clear.

The prophesied earthly kingdom program is all about Israel's rise; but during this time of the Mystery, blessings come as a result of Israel's fall.

Zechariah 8:23: Thus saith the LORD of hosts; In those days it shall come to pass, that ten men shall take hold out of all languages of the nations, even shall take hold of the skirt of him that is a Jew, saying, We will go with you: for we have heard that God is with you.

Genesis 12:2-3: And I will make of thee a great nation, and I will bless thee, and make thy name great; and thou shalt be a blessing: And I will bless them that bless thee, and curse him that curseth thee: and in thee shall all families of the earth be blessed.

Note the difference:

Romans 11:11-12: ...through their fall salvation is come unto the Gentiles, for to provoke them to jealousy. Now if the fall of them be the riches of the world, and the diminishing of them the riches of the Gentiles; how much more their fulness?

Romans 11:15: For if the casting away of them be the reconciling of the world, what shall the receiving of them be, but life from the dead?

The ramification of Israel's fall, diminishing and casting away is that, in Christ according to the Mystery, Israel has no standing whatsoever.

Romans 12:10: Be kindly affectioned one to another with brotherly love; in honour preferring one another;

Romans 3:22: Even the righteousness of God which is by faith of Jesus Christ unto all and upon all them that believe: for there is no difference:

Galatians 3:28: There is neither Jew nor Greek, there is neither bond nor free, there is neither male nor female: for ye are all one in Christ Jesus.

I Corinthians 12:13: For by one Spirit are we all baptized into one body, whether we be Jews or Gentiles, whether we be bond or free; and have been all made to drink into one Spirit.

Since Christianity is according to the revelation of the mystery and since both the Old and New Testaments deal with Israel and that nation's prophesied kingdom, for one to call himself or herself a "New Testament Christian" is to butcher the word of truth rather than to rightly divide it.

The most important things we can learn as we study the Bible are the differences between the Prophecy and the Mystery programs. The two edged sword of the word of truth can do a lot of damage in the hands of the novice or the apprentice. The workman that needeth not to be ashamed will be the one who cuts straight, rightly dividing Mystery from Prophecy.

---

1. I Corinthians 15:40 There are also celestial bodies, and bodies terrestrial: but the glory of the celestial is one, and the glory of the terrestrial is another.

2. Ephesians 1:3 Blessed be the God and Father of our Lord Jesus Christ, who hath blessed us with all spiritual blessings in heavenly places in Christ:

Colossians 1:16 For by him were all things created, that are in heaven, and that are in earth, visible and invisible, whether they be thrones, or dominions, or principalities, or powers: all things were created by him, and for him:

The Hebrew epistles...
belong to the Hebrews

Before Peter or John wrote their Hebrew epistles, they met with Paul and Barnabas. At that meeting, in addition to setting aside the so-called "great commissions" found in the four gospels, they determined that Peter, James and John would confine their ministries to the circumcision.

Galatians 2:9: And when <u>James, Cephas, and John</u>, who seemed to be pillars, perceived the grace that was given unto me, they gave to me and Barnabas the right hands of fellowship; that we should go unto the heathen, and <u>they unto the circumcision.</u>

There is no need to appeal to commentaries or church tradition to discern the audience and intent of the Hebrew epistles. What is necessary is to realize that Israel is the recipient of the prophecy program, the covenants belong to Israel, and the Hebrew epistles are aimed at instructing Israel on how to endure until the end of the tribulation and to enter into Israel's millennial kingdom.

Matthew 24:13: But he that shall endure unto the end, the same shall be saved.

Matthew 24:21: For then shall be great tribulation, such as was not since the beginning of the world to this time, no, nor ever shall be.

One might surmise that calling a book "Hebrews" would make it clear to all that the content would be to and about the Hebrew people. Perhaps many were led astray by Dr. C. I. Scofield's note that the book was written to "Jewish Christians."[1] Since we know from the twenty-eighth verse of Galatians chapter three that *"There is neither Jew nor Greek"* in the body of Christ, it is apparent that Scofield's note engenders confusion rather than clarity.

That the book of Hebrews is not written to the body of Christ in this dispensation is clear when we note that the audience for the book is the same people who were present in the four gospels and at Pentecost:

> *Hebrews 2:3-4: How shall we escape, if we neglect so great salvation; which at the first began to be spoken by the Lord, and was confirmed unto us by them that heard him; God also bearing them witness, both with signs and wonders, and with divers miracles, and gifts of the Holy Ghost, according to his own will?*

Another easily discerned fact is that the book of Hebrews confirms God's new covenant promise to Israel, almost exactly as God first stated it in the old covenant:

> *Jeremiah 31:31: Behold, the days come, saith the LORD, that <u>I will make a new covenant with the house of Israel, and with the house of Judah:</u>*
> *Hebrews 8:8: For finding fault with them, he saith, Behold, the days come, saith the Lord, when <u>I will make a new</u>*

covenant with the house of Israel and with the house of Judah:

Problem passages in the book of Hebrews are easily understood when we realize the audience for the book is the Hebrew people either in the Tribulation or in their new covenant.

James is even easier.

James 1:1: James, a servant of God and of the Lord Jesus Christ, to the twelve tribes which are scattered abroad, greeting.

While people debate which James wrote the book, it wouldn't matter if your name were James and you wrote it last week: what matters is the doctrinal content and the audience to which the doctrine is directed.

Not only do we know James was written to the twelve tribes of Israel, we know when because the tribes were scattered in Acts chapter eight, while Paul was yet Saul and the mystery was yet hidden.

Acts 8:1: And Saul was consenting unto his death. And at that time there was a great persecution against the church which was at Jerusalem; and they were all scattered abroad throughout the regions of Judaea and Samaria, except the apostles.

With the mystery still hidden because Christ had not yet converted Saul to Paul and given the mystery to him, James talks about works and religion as you would expect a Hebrew to talk to Israel.

Peter, having the keys to the kingdom

since Matthew sixteen, having delivered the message on the day of Pentecost, writes two epistles to his people Israel.

Were Peter talking to Gentiles, he could not say:

I Peter 2:12: Having your conversation honest among the Gentiles...

And if that weren't enough, Peter speaks of salvation delivered at the second coming of Christ, exactly as he had done on the day of Pentecost.[2]

I Peter 1:13: Wherefore gird up the loins of your mind, be sober, and hope to the end for the grace that is to be brought unto you at the revelation of Jesus Christ;

The three epistles of John all speak to commandment keeping and knowing the reader's relationship with God is acceptable based upon performance: hardly a message of grace through faith. The verses are too numerous to list, but here are some of the most salient examples:

I John 2:3-4: And hereby we do know that we know him, if we keep his commandments. He that saith, I know him, and keepeth not his commandments, is a liar, and the truth is not in him.

I John 3:22: And whatsoever we ask, we receive of him, because we keep his commandments, and do those things that are pleasing in his sight.

Ask the next person who claims the doctrines in John's Hebrew epistles how getting whatsoever they ask is working out for them. While these little letters have much to say on a spiritual level about love and fellowship, clearly the doctrine belongs to new covenant Israel.

In Second John it remains the law program as given by the Father, not the grace program as given by Christ to Paul:

> *II John 4: I rejoiced greatly that I found of thy children walking in truth, as we have received a commandment from the Father.*

The "elect lady" will be the "Israel mine elect,"[3] and since the focus is "that which ye have heard from the beginning"[4] it could not be that which shows up with the revelation of the mystery, Acts chapter nine and after.

Jude is an epistle given little attention by most people except for two or three verses used as slogans. Meanwhile, the book of Jude is replete with Old Testament references applied to Israel's New Testament promises.

Note also that Jude deals with the words of the apostles in verse seventeen and people who can fall in verse twenty-four: hardly mystery truth, certainly not "complete in Christ" and "sealed unto the day of redemption."[5]

And finally we come to the last of the Hebrew epistles, the book of Revelation, about which much more wrong has been taught than that which would be correct.

Revelation is all about the time of Jacob's trouble, Daniel's seventieth week, the great tribulation. Clearly, the book of Revelation is prophecy and relates to Old Testament prophecy, most particularly Ezekiel and Daniel. That alone should be sufficient for us to realize Revelation would not contain mystery truth for the body of Christ, spiritualized preaching on the first three chapters notwithstanding.

Trying to combine doctrine from the book of Revelation with Pauline truth is so painfully wrong that doing so has been the source of two cults: Seventh Day Adventism and the World Wide Church of God. Both hold to Revelation's "everlasting gospel" *"which keep the commandments of God, and have the testimony of Jesus Christ."* (*Revelation 12:17, 14:6*)

To make it as simple as possible, Revelation chapter five verse ten identifies that this book of prophecy could not be intended as doctrine for those of us who are going to heaven:

> *Revelation 5:10: And hast made us unto our God kings and priests: and we shall reign on the earth.*

That Revelation belongs to Israel is hard for many believers to accept because it is so exciting to think that we are seeing prophecy fulfilled in our lifetimes. Many see the difference between "law" and "grace" but resist accepting the difference between "prophecy" and "mystery." Be that as it may, we must preach Christ according to the revelation of the mystery or be wrong: it is as simple as that.

The Hebrew epistles then, explain to Israel the benefits of their Messiah's cross and help them to prepare for their time of tribulation and their kingdom on this Earth.

They make for interesting reading to be sure, and a good source for some spiritual truth and definition of terms; but they have no doctrinal application for the Body of Christ, save when they agree with our apostle, Paul.

---

1. Scofield Study Bible, Dr. C. I. Scofield, Oxford Publishing Company, page 1291

2. *Acts 3:19 Repent ye therefore, and be converted, that your sins may be blotted out, when the times of refreshing shall come from the presence of the Lord.*

3. *Isaiah 45:4 For Jacob my servant's sake, and Israel mine elect, I have even called thee by thy name: I have surnamed thee, though thou hast not known me.*

4. II John 6 And this is love, that we walk after his commandments. This is the commandment, That, as ye have heard from the beginning, ye should walk in it.

5. Colossians 2:10 And ye are complete in him, which is the head of all principality and power:

Ephesians 4:30 And grieve not the holy Spirit of God, whereby ye are sealed unto the day of redemption.

We obey the Lord Jesus Christ when we follow Paul...

WWJD, "What would Jesus do?," was a very popular fad for a time, the thinking based upon Charles Sheldon's book <u>In His Steps</u>, the theme of which being that to follow the Lord Jesus' life example is what it means to be a Christian.

Not only is such thinking wrong in regards to salvation because it requires works rather than grace and faith, it is also wrong to think that we should follow the Lord when the Lord Himself would have us to follow Paul and Pauline doctrine according to the revelation of the mystery.

Jesus said:

John 13:20: Verily, verily, I say unto you, He that receiveth whomsoever I send receiveth me; and he that receiveth me receiveth him that sent me.

We can make no mistake about it: the Lord Jesus Christ sent Paul just as certainly as Jehovah sent Moses:

I Corinthians 14:37: ...the things that I write unto you are the commandments of the Lord.

Ephesians 3:2: ...the dispensation of the grace of God which is given me to

you-ward:
Acts 26:16: But rise, and stand upon thy feet: for I have appeared unto thee for this purpose, to make thee a minister and a witness both of these things which thou hast seen, and of those things in the which I will appear unto thee;
Romans 11:13: For I speak to you Gentiles, inasmuch as I am the apostle of the Gentiles, I magnify mine office:
1 Timothy 1:16: Howbeit for this cause I obtained mercy, that in me first Jesus Christ might shew forth all longsuffering, for a pattern to them which should hereafter believe on him to life everlasting.

When we take the attitude that the Bible is right and what we might have heard or might have thought must always submit to Bible truth, our belief system becomes a product of the Bible itself rather than what may have been said or thought about the Bible.

Granted, it sounds wrong, even blasphemous to some, to say that we get our marching orders from Paul. Have you ever heard anyone suggest that Israel was wrong to follow Moses? Has anyone ever accused the Hebrew people of worshiping Moses? Of course not.

This, however, is different and we would do well to understand the difference. Red letters in millions of Bibles wrongly elevated Jesus' words over the rest of the words in the Bible. We refer to ourselves as

"Christians" and He is our Saviour, so it is a very natural thing to desire to obey Him; and by common understanding it would seem a lessening of Christ's preeminence to follow Paul.

To follow and obey the Lord Jesus while disregarding what the Lord Jesus said would be folly; but that is where most church-going people who call themselves "Christian" find themselves.

First, the Lord tells Ananias in a vision that He has chosen Paul to go to the Gentiles:

Acts 9:15: But the Lord said unto him, Go thy way: for he is a chosen vessel unto me, to bear my name before the Gentiles, and kings, and the children of Israel:

Even as Paul was being attacked and threatened by a mob in Jerusalem, Paul gives testimony to Christ's instructions:

Acts 22:21: And he said unto me, Depart: for I will send thee far hence unto the Gentiles.

Perhaps the most clear exposition and explanation of what Christ said to Paul in Acts chapter nine is given seventeen chapters later when Paul stands before Agrippa and describes his encounter with the Lord:

Acts 26:15-17 And I said, Who art thou, Lord? And he said, I am Jesus whom thou persecutest. But rise, and stand upon thy feet: for I have appeared unto thee for this purpose, to make thee a minister and a witness both of these things which thou hast seen, and of those things in the which I will appear unto thee; Delivering thee from the people, and from the Gentiles, unto whom now I send thee,

Note also that Jesus promised to contact Paul subsequently and more than once when Christ told Paul to be alert to *"those things in the which I will appear unto thee"* in verse sixteen above. This bit of detail helps us understand how Paul knew more mystery information later in his life then at the beginning, when Paul still thought as a child and saw through the glass darkly. The fact that Paul could say *"Christ sent me not to baptize[1]"* after Paul had been baptizing makes it evident that baptism was not a subject covered in Acts nine but a subject clearly dealt with by the time Paul wrote his first Corinthian epistle.

Paul declared that the Lord Jesus sent him to be a light unto the Gentiles; and if Paul is the Lord's choice, who are we to argue?

Acts 13:46-47: Then Paul and Barnabas waxed bold, and said, It was necessary that the word of God should first have been spoken to you: but seeing ye put it from you, and judge yourselves unworthy of everlasting life, lo, we turn to the Gentiles. For so hath the Lord commanded us, saying, I have set thee to be a light of the Gentiles, that thou shouldest be for salvation unto the ends of the earth.

When our Bible gives us definition, we

need not look elsewhere. Rather than trying to interpret and evaluate Bible verses using external sources, we would be wise if we evaluated everything else by our Bible. Many people pore over commentaries, and if you asked them what they are doing, they would tell you they are studying the Bible: in actuality they are reading books about the Bible, and that is not Bible study.

Note the unambiguous definition the Bible gives us describing the ministry of the Lord Jesus Christ and then eight verses later defining and describing Paul's ministry:

> *Romans 15:8: Now I say that Jesus Christ was a minister of the circumcision for the truth of God, to confirm the promises made unto the fathers:*
> *Romans 15:16: That I should be the minister of Jesus Christ to the Gentiles, ministering the gospel of God, that the offering up of the Gentiles might be acceptable, being sanctified by the Holy Ghost.*

Christ, minister of the circumcision; Paul, minister of the Gentiles: exactly as Peter, James and John went to the circumcision and Paul to the Gentiles:

> *Galatians 2:7: But contrariwise, when they saw that the gospel of the uncircumcision was committed unto me, as the gospel of the circumcision was unto Peter;*

Paul was the last to see the Lord Jesus, the first to get the message of longsuffering grace and the pattern to all of us who are believers:

*I Corinthians 15:8: And <u>last of all he
was seen of me</u> also, as of one born
out of due time.*

*I Timothy 1:16: Howbeit for this cause I
obtained mercy, <u>that in me first</u> Jesus
Christ might shew forth all longsuffering, for <u>a pattern to them which should
hereafter believe on him to life everlasting.</u>*

The dispensation of the grace of God
and the revelation of the mystery were committed to Paul by our Lord Jesus Christ.

*Ephesians 3:2: If ye have heard of the
dispensation of the grace of God which
is given me to you-ward:*

*Ephesians 3:7: Whereof I was made a
minister, according to the gift of the
grace of God given unto me by the ef-
fectual working of his power.*

*Colossians 1:25-26: Whereof I am
made a minister, according to the dispensation of God which is given to me
for you, to fulfil the word of God; Even
the mystery which hath been hid from
ages and from generations, but now is
made manifest to his saints:*

Since Peter, James, John and the apostles of the four gospels had restricted their
ministry to the circumcision, what they did
and said would be consistent with what the
Lord Jesus did and said during His earthly
ministry, with Paul and Barnabas going to
the uncircumcision.[2] Small wonder then,
that the Lord delegated preaching the mystery to Paul; for were the Lord to preach the
mystery Himself, it would create conflicts

and confusion with what had happened and been taught (by the same Lord) according to prophecy in the four gospels.

Because Peter and the eleven apostles confined their ministries to the circumcision, Paul became the only teacher of the Gentiles:

> I Timothy 2:7: Whereunto I am ordained a preacher, and an apostle, (I speak the truth in Christ, and lie not;) a teacher of the Gentiles in faith and verity.

> II Timothy 1:11: Whereunto I am appointed a preacher, and an apostle, and a teacher of the Gentiles.

When Paul began his life in Christ in Acts nine, Paul was separated unto the Gentiles as their sole minister. When Paul was near the end of his life on earth and ready to be offered, Paul still focused on his Gentile ministry:

> II Timothy 4:17: Notwithstanding the Lord stood with me, and strengthened me; that by me the preaching might be fully known, and that all the Gentiles might hear: and I was delivered out of the mouth of the lion.

We should not be any harder on others than we would be hard on ourselves for having missed or having rejected the importance of being Pauline in our doctrine. Millions who have gone before us and millions who will follow after us have been turned from Paul's writings by the error-prone traditions that permeate practicing Christianity. We are wise if we avoid the trap of making a career out of telling everyone what is wrong:

better we show people the rightness of being Pauline with simple and clear verses:

II Corinthians 4:15-16: For though ye have ten thousand instructors in Christ, yet have ye not many fathers: for in Christ Jesus I have begotten you through the gospel. Wherefore I beseech you, be ye followers of me.

I Corinthians 11:1: Be ye followers of me, even as I also am of Christ.

I Corinthians 14:37: If any man think himself to be a prophet, or spiritual, let him acknowledge that the things that I write unto you are the commandments of the Lord.

Romans 16:17-18: Now I beseech you, brethren, mark them which cause divisions and offences contrary to the doctrine which ye have learned; and avoid them. For they that are such serve not our Lord Jesus Christ, but their own belly; and by good words and fair speeches deceive the hearts of the simple.

There are preachers that can get you so fired up you are ready to charge hell with a squirt gun full of gasoline. There are books you can read that grab your emotional handles and won't turn them loose. There are singers who can put tears in your eyes and musicians who can put a song in your heart.

That being the case, we must discipline ourselves to be focused on Pauline doctrine and the preaching according to the revelation of the mystery.

No matter how wonderful or convincing prophecy preaching and messianic messages may sound, we must never forget that those doctrines belong to Israel.

Philippians 3:17-19: Brethren, be followers together of me, and mark them which walk so as ye have us for an ensample. (For many walk, of whom I have told you often, and now tell you even weeping, that they are the enemies of the cross of Christ: Whose end is destruction, whose God is their belly, and whose glory is in their shame, who mind earthly things.)

Sad to say, the enemies of the cross in the passage just above are the same people who are enemies of the Gospel in Romans;[3] Israel, the circumcision. And it follows as night follows day that even now those church-goers who think they are Israel, (the circumcision, the priesthood of believers), are enemies of the gospel of the grace of God.

The grace of God.

The grace of God by unmerited favor, unknown under the law.

The grace of God apart from performance, unknown in the gospels.

The grace of God which had never been shown forth until Paul gave testimony, in due time.[4]

If the Lord Jesus Christ were to answer the question, "What would Jesus do?" the Lord would send you to Paul's writings and the revelation of the mystery, *"…as though God did beseech you by us." (II Corinthians 15:19).*

II Timothy 1:8 Be not thou therefore ashamed of the testimony of our Lord, nor of me his prisoner: but be thou partaker of the afflictions of the gospel according to the power of God;

---

1. *I Corinthians 1:17 For Christ sent me not to baptize, but to preach the gospel: not with wisdom of words, lest the cross of Christ should be made of none effect.*

2. *Galatians 2:9 And when James, Cephas, and John, who seemed to be pillars, perceived the grace that was given unto me, they gave to me and Barnabas the right hands of fellowship; that we should go unto the heathen, and they unto the circumcision.*

3. *Romans 11:26-28 And so all Israel shall be saved: as it is written, There shall come out of Sion the Deliverer, and shall turn away ungodliness from Jacob: For this is my covenant unto them, when I shall take away their sins. As concerning the gospel, they are enemies for your sakes: but as touching the election, they are beloved for the fathers' sakes.*

4. *1 Timothy 2:6 Who gave himself a ransom for all, to be testified in due time.*

Epilogue...

While this book was a "work in progress" it was referred to as B-MAD which is the acronym for its title: <u>Basics of Mid-Acts Dispensationalism</u>.

B-MAD also works on some other levels:

You should be mad (B-MAD) if you were never taught the concept of Mid-Acts Dispensationalism before now. Whether you agree with the concepts or not, you should not have been kept in ignorance.

You may be mad (B-MAD) now that you have learned what Mid-Acts Dispensationalism is because it is so devastating to covenant and/or denominational thinking.

Should you teach Mid-Acts Dispensationalism to others, those people might say (with apologies to Acts 26:24) "Much learning doth make thee (be) mad."

Winston Churchill once observed, "Men occasionally stumble over truth, but most of them pick themselves up and hurry off as if nothing happened."

Generally speaking, when a person knowingly rejects truth it is because truth hurts and Mid-Acts Dispensational truth would hurt income, position, reputation or associations.

Ultimately, we must each *"be fully persuaded in his own mind." (Romans 14:5)*

Just don't be mad. Rather, *Study to shew thyself approved unto God, rightly dividing the word of truth. (II Timothy 2:15)*

How does a person get to heaven? Follow Patty through her neighborhood as she keeps asking her most important question until she gets the right answer.

This book is an outstanding evangelistic tool that you can give to every child you know.

Just 32 pages of well written and beautifully illustrated material making the gospel of the Grace of God clear and accessible.

- Order one copy for $3 retail plus actual postage of $1.35, total $4.35
- Order five copies for $15 and we pay postage.
- Ten for $30, fifteen for $45, and we pay postage.
- Order in multiples of Twenty for $50, (forty for $100, sixty for $150 and so on)

Mail your check or money order to:
Discerning the Times Publishing Co. Inc.
Post Office Box 87, Alpha OH 45301

The "With A Bible In My Hand" weekly newspaper column first appeared in August of 1988 in the *Beavercreek Current* and was subsequently and simultaneously published in the:

Greene Country Messenger
Christian News
Pulpit Helps
Beavercreek News-Current
Dayton Daily News
Christian Free Press
Voice in the Wilderness
Christ & Country Courier

The final "With A Bible In My Hand" column was published in October, 1999, with more than 700 columns in print.

"With A Bible In My Hand" was awarded three prestigious Amy Awards for excellence in Christian writing in the secular press and the Founder of the Amy Foundation cited "With A Bible In My Hand" columns in his book. Twice the Ohio State Legislature cited columnist Terence D. McLean as "one of Ohio's finest citizens," because of "insightful and extraordinary...positive contributions."

The Greene County Foster Children's Picnic was fostered by the column as it gave awareness that Bible-Believing fundamentalist Christians actually have something to say and to contribute to the marketplace of ideas. McLean has been listed among "Who's Who In American Religion" since 1982.

Order one copy for $6 retail
    plus postage of $1.59, total $7.59
•Order five copies for $30 and we pay (U,S.) postage.
•Ten for $60, fifteen for $90, we pay (U.S.) postage.
    Larger orders save one dollar per book:
•Order in multiples of Twenty for $100, (forty for $200, sixty for $300 and so on), we pay (U.S.) postage.

Send your check or money order to:
discerning the times publishing co. inc.
Post Office Box 87
Alpha OH 45301-0087

Newly published is this marvelous group of nine of Dr. C.I. Scofield's sermons with annotations demonstrating just how far Dispensationalism has come since his time.

Sermon titles include:
  The Inner Life
  The Imparted Life
  The Tragedy of
    the Inner Life
  The Delivered Life
  The Larger Christian Life
  The Spirit Controlled Life
  The Joyous Life
  True Consecration
  Defilement and Cleansing

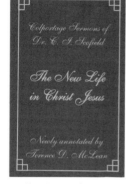

The New Life in Jesus Christ is a compilation of messages preached by Dr. Scofield to his congregations at Dallas, Texas and Northfield, Massachusetts. These were published in the "Christian Worker's Magazine" and then published in book form by the Bible Institute Colportage Association in 1915. These messages, subtitled 'Messages of Joy and Victory' are republished now in the spirit of Dr. Scofield's dedication, in that first edition:

"This book is here and now committed to the care of Him whom it seeks to exalt in the fervent prayer that through His grace it may show the way into happy, victorious, fruitful Christian living to many in bondage."

        Reading this book is to stand on the shoulders of a giant and to see God's provision for our new life in Christ Jesus...

Order one copy for $5 retail
        plus postage of $1.59, total $6.59
•Order five copies for $25 and we pay (U,S.) postage.
•Ten for $50, fifteen for $75, we pay (U.S.) postage.
•Order in multiples of Twenty for $80, (forty for $160, sixty for $240 and so on).

Send your check or money order to:
discerning the times publishing co. inc.
Post Office Box 87
Alpha OH 45301-0087